LUCIANA SAVELLI

Photos: NICOLA GRIFONI and JOSÉ GOMES

OPORTO
NORTHERN PORTUGAL

300 COLOR PHOTOGRAPHS

OPORTO CITY MAP

VILA NOVA DE GAIA
VILA DO CONDE
PÓVOA DE VARZIM
VIANA DO CASTELO
BARCELOS
CITÂNIA DE BRITEIROS
BRAGA
BOM JESUS DO MONTE
GUIMARÃES
VILA REAL
AMARANTE
AVEIRO
CONÍMBRIGA
COIMBRA
FIGUEIRA DA FOZ

BONECHI EDIZIONI "IL TURISMO"

Imported by:
DISTRI-CULTURAL - SOCIEDADE DIFUSORA DE CULTURA, LDA.
Rua Vasco da Gama, Nr 4/4A • P-2686-969 Sacavém - Lisboa

Exclusive distributor for Portugal:
ELECTROLIBER, LDA.
Central & Southern: Rua Vasco da Gama, Nr 4/4A
                    P-2686-969 Sacavém - Lisboa
                    Tel: +351-219406500 • Fax: +351-219425214
Northern: Rua da Boavista, Nr 382 • P-4415-549 Grijo
          Tel: +351-227452190 • Fax: +351-227648620

Publishing manager: Barbara Bonechi
Publishing coordinator and text editor: Lorena Lazzari
Graphics and layout: Paola Rufino
English translation: Studio Comunicare, Florence
Photo credits: Nicola Grifoni (photographic service specially carried out
for the Publishing House)
Interior and works of art photos: José Gomes Ferreira
Photo on page 121: Massimo Listri
Photolithography: Bluprint Srl., Florence
Printing: Grafedit Spa., Azzano S. Paolo (Bergamo)
ISBN: 88-7204-486-3

The texts in the boxes "*Talha Dourada*" and "*Museums of Oporto*" were
written by Alessandro Listri

Particular thanks go to Benedetta Listri, for her invaluable collaboration

The Oporto city map was made available by the Culture Department of
the Oporto City Council

* The location of the works given is where they where when the book went to press

WELCOME TO NORTHERN PORTUGAL

There are specific differences and contrasts between Northern and Southern Portugal, in climate, vegetation, cuisine, customs, history, characteristics of austerity and mildness. The North is a region that is still growing economically, with proud but hospitable towns, farmers, fishermen and craftsmen who live and work in the traditional industriousness of the northern peoples, even though Portugal as a whole belongs to Southern Europe.

The panorama of the North is varied: morphologically mountainous and wilder the *Trás-os-Montes* "behind the mountains", green and rainy the *Minho*, the most flourishing region of Portugal, on the border with Spanish Galicia, with the cities of Guimarães, Barcelos, Braga; with extensive fine beaches on the ocean, such as Vila do Conde, Oporto, Vila Praia de Âncora. There are a wealth of streams and long rivers such as the Minho, the Douro, and the blue Rio Lima, the only one which has its source in Portugal, and which charmed the Romans who saw it as that mythological Lethe River which made anyone who dipped into its waters lose their memory.

The North is not densely populated – with the exception of Aveiro, Coimbra, Oporto and Braga, where between the 1960s and the 1980s a million and more Portuguese left Lusitania, above all for France. Every summer these immigrants return home to take part in weddings, since August is the month for weddings. And they come back forever, once they retire, and build a house. Now the many indus-

tries that have been created here have reduced emigration, providing work in the textile factories, iron and steel works, fisheries, cosmetics, wine cellars. The flourishing crafts are another important element in the North. Despite all this the peasant origins keep the North closely tied to its traditions, folklore, religious practices (Braga, known as the Lusitanian Rome). The *Trás-os-Montes* was the traditional refuge of reli-

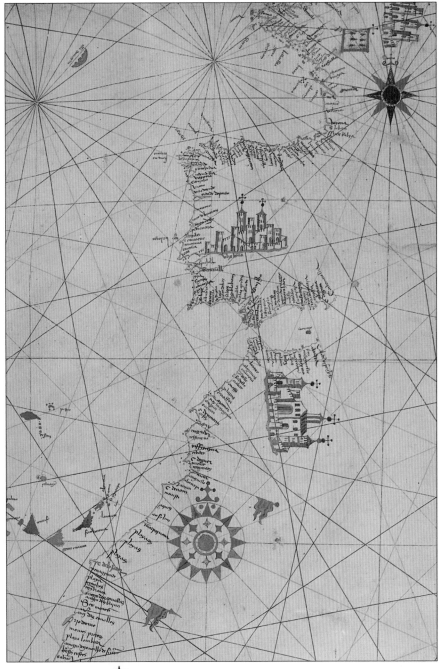

▶ *An old nautical map showing the coast of Portugal*

gious and political exiles. The *Romarias*, religious festivals dedicated to the patron saint, which end in dances, music and banquets, are also very much felt.

The cuisine of the North is more rustic than that of the rest of Portugal. Butter is one of the principal ingredients, with pork, kid and beans. This is the homeland of many national dishes, such as the *caldo verde*, *bacalhau* (dried salted cod, called *fiel amigo*, faithful friend), and salmon from the Minho. And then the good wine, the *vinho verde*, or the *Dão*, and the famous *Port wine* produced in the Upper Douro, which began to be sold in Viana do Castelo, a city on the Atlantic coast.

The North was the land of the Lusitani, that is the famous Celtiberian tribe, led by Viriathus, the first national Portuguese hero, who resisted before surrendering to the Romans. Citânia de Briteiros is one of the most important archaeological sites, situated between Braga and Guimarães, and still has traces of these peoples from whom the Portuguese descend. The birth of Portugal, as a race and as a nation, took place in the North, in the region between the Minho and the Douro, entrusted to Henry of Burgundy in 1095 by his father in law Alfonso VI of León and Castile. It was Henry of Burgundy who initiated the founding of an independent kingdom, for he supported the archbishops of Braga in freeing themselves from the tutelage of Toledo and Santiago de Compostela. His son, Prince Afonso Henriques, known as

the Conqueror, consecrated the independence of the realm in 1142 at the time of the *Reconquista*. There is a reason why the words "*Aqui nasceu Portugal*" are written on the medieval walls of Guimarães.

The era of discoveries also began in the North, in the city of Oporto, thanks to Henry the Navigator, son of King João I, conqueror of Ceuta. It was Henry who started the policy which provided the means to finance ocean voyages of discovery, thanks to their administration of the property of the Order of Christ.

Much of Portuguese culture comes from the North too and the cradle and center is in the city of Coimbra, above all in the excellent university.

Again it is the North which can boast of that particular type of carved and gilded decoration, the *talha dourada*, which adorns so many churches and cathedrals with its extraordinary Baroque feeling.

Visiting Northern Portugal is a fascinating trip full of unexpected emotions for even the most jaded traveler. All the more so since the region has countless hotels and restaurants and the most charming *pousadas*, villas and convents equipped with the latest modern comforts. The specific type of farm holiday tourism known as *turismo de habitação* is also well developed, with elegantly furnished old patrician dwellings and mansions with their fragrant gardens ready to welcome the guests.

OPORTO

An old proverb runs "Lisbon has a good time, Braga prays, Coimbra studies and Oporto works". This really seems to be the case. Oporto is a working city, enterprising, hard, commercial, industrial, modern, buzzing with maritime river trade, with a great port, the Leixões, and five hundred thousand inhabitants which reach a million or more if you count in the entire district.

It shares the role of industrial capital of Lusitania as well as that of a rich, beautiful and fascinating city with Lisbon, its eternal "rival". Observing the city carefully from up on the Dom Luís I Bridge one can get an idea of what Lisbon must have been like before the earthquake. The inhabitants of Oporto don't like comparisons with Lisbon, if such a thing is possible. They simply don't like it.

Porto is the original name and not Oporto as foreigners often say, with the "O Porto" the name the English used to indicate the wine still ringing in their ears. But it was thanks to this wine that the economy of Oporto got a new lease on life after trade in spices went into a decline.

At first sight, the city could be compared to a mysterious beautiful lady, hoarding a wealth of historical and cultural memories, making no show of her charm, and not interested in conventions, but cultivating her vocation for pragmatism. Once the initial mistrust has been overcome, Oporto opens its doors and does not fail to comply with the expectations and curiosity of the visitor. Its heart has always retained the down-to-earth quality of plain folk bound to traditions, with a pleasure-seeking vein which comes to life in the evening after work is done and during the many festivals scattered through the Portuguese calendar. And Oporto really goes wild rooting for its soccer squad for which the *Antas*, a modern stadium, has been built.

They all say it is the loveliest city in Portugal. In 1996 UNESCO declared it a World Heritage Site, and it has been declared the European capital of culture for the year 2001. The city prepared for the great event by refurbishing its palaces, churches and streets.

Oporto is rich in contrasts, polyhedral, proud, frenetic, with a chaotic and fast moving traffic where

◄ *Dom Luís I Bridge and the roofs of the Fontainhas district*

honking your horn seems to be unheard of. But if you go towards the Ribeira, in the popular districts along the Douro River, you find yourself in another world, another period, enveloped in mystery and *Saudade* where time seems almost to be standing still.

Oporto is called the city of granite, for almost every building is in stone and iron, softened by the azulejos. The bridges, the austere medieval Baroque and modern buildings which give no hint of their sumptuous interiors, make the city look austere and gray. But there is also magic there, especially in the morning or at dusk when a thick fog rises from the Ocean and envelops the city, till the sun disperses the mists and brings out the luminous pastel colors of the Ribeira and the azulejos found outside as well as inside churches and palaces.

Oporto is known as the city of the *tripeiros*, tripe eaters, as they are called in Lisbon, and the inhabitants of Oporto who really know how to cook take no offense and remind the *Lisboetas*, that in the fifteenth century, when Prince Henry the Navigator weighed anchor for an expedition to Africa, opening the way to the discoveries, it was they who offered the *Infante*, their fellow citizen, the best meat in the city, and kept only tripe for themselves. Oporto moreover enjoys a good gastronomic reputation, with a varied cuisine of meat and fish. In addition to the renowned tripe, another dish has been made famous by literature, the *sarrabulho*, a mixture of pork and beef and fowl,

▼ *Panorama of the city and the double loop of the Douro River*

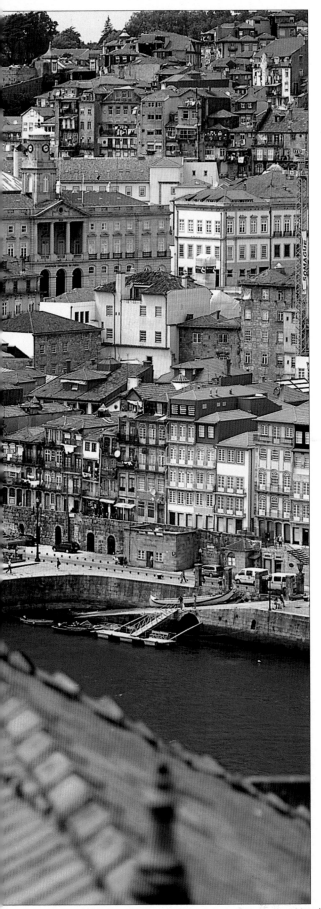

cut in small pieces and cooked with rice, spices and herbs. It is one of those dishes so appetizing that the Portuguese writer José Saramago called it "one of those dishes which nourishes the body and consoles the spirit". A must in Oporto is chocolate, prepared in a thousand ways with Brazilian cocoa, such as the superb chocolates in elegant boxes in the famous shop in the *Arcádia* in *Avenida dos Aliados*.

By vocation and by history it is an independent and liberal city, with the cult of freedom, a city that is bourgeois and of the bourgeoisie, never noble and never coveted by the aristocrats. In far off 1628 the women rose up against the minister of Finances because of an exceedingly high tax on linen, and in 1810 the city went all out for the Republican revolts, and was one of the first to rebel against Napoleon. And it seems only yesterday that Lisbon took part in the Revolution of the Carnations in 1974.

Oporto and Braga vie with each other for the title of capital of the Baroque, with their many sumptuous, opulent Baroque churches laden with gold.

The city is on the right bank of the Douro River, to which Oporto owes its fortune, five kilometers from the mouth in the stretch where the river curves twice forming a sinuous meander. The city looks like an amphitheater with the houses shouldering each other as they climb vertically up the hill of Pena Ventosa, with its steep streets, a real challenge to whoever explores the town on foot.

On the other bank of the Douro, the suburb of Vila Nova de Gaia looks over at Oporto. It is the sacred place of wine and wine lodges, situated one next to the other and most of them still controlled by the English. Another aspect of the city is the marked acculturation with the English with whom agreements were stipulated in far distant 1352. Nor must Brazil be forgotten, to which Oporto is profoundly tied as a sort of second homeland. The custom of facing the exteriors of buildings with azulejos to enjoy their beauty all the more is typically Brazilian.

Oporto is an ancient city, but with an extraordinary capacity for renewal, promotion and daring. Take the use of iron in building the *Dona Maria Pia* and *Dom Luís I* bridges and in the futuristic architecture of Álvaro Siza Vieira in his *Casa de Chá da Boa Nova*, a large restaurant bar, a magnificent structure in the mist of the rocks which move down towards the Ocean.

◀ *The Ribeira district*

The Dom Luís I Bridge

Oporto has four bridges and a fifth is under construction. But the bridge which is a landmark and unmistakable feature of the city is the daring nineteenth century Dom Luís I Bridge. A gigantic road bridge in iron, elegant and harmonious, on two levels and with a single archway, it joins the historical districts, upper and lower, of Oporto with those of Vila Nova de Gaia. This magnificent work of engineering, suspended seventy meters over the river, was designed in 1886 by the Portuguese Teófilo Seyring and built by the Belgian firm Willebroeck on the lines of Gustave Eiffel's Dona Maria Pia railroad

bridge of a few years earlier. The upper level, which leads to the upper districts, is three hundred ninety-two meters long, while the lower one measures a hundred seventy-four meters in length. Each level has two-way traffic and two sidewalks. Walking across the bridge on foot is a fascinating but challenging undertaking with cars racing by all around. But it is worth it, for the view over the river and the city from here is superb.

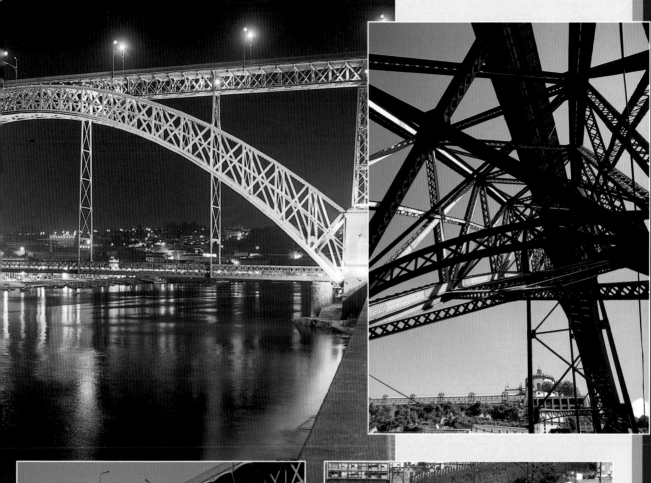

Oporto already existed as a village in the eighth century B.C., the Iron age, and traded with the Hellenes along the Mediterranean. Originally it was called Cale on the left bank of the river, while the Romans built Portus on the right bank. It became one of the most strategic settlements of the Empire in Lusitania, and trade grew and the city began to grow rich and became Portu Cale. It was then conquered by the Suebi and the Visigoths, to fall under the Moors in 750. In 850 it became Christian once more. From then on the story of Portu Cale coincides with that of Portucalense or Portugal. The city became capital of the county of León, the region between the Minho and Douro rivers, and became independent after the marriage of Henry of Burgundy in 1095 with Dona Teresa, the daughter of the king of León and Castile, Alfonso VI. Their son was Afonso Henriques, first king of Portugal, who defeated the Arabs in the Chris-

tian *Reconquista*. Oporto became ever more important and in the fifteenth century Prince Henry the Navigator, their fellow citizen, opened the way to maritime discoveries and subsequently to the economic apogee. In 1703 Oporto signed the Methuen Treaty guaranteeing the English the rights to trade in wool in Portugal and providing the Portuguese with a ready market for their *Port wine* in England. When Marquês de Pombal, prime minister of King

José I, applied a stricter control on the commerce of wine to contrast the English monopoly, the producers rebelled and governmental repression was harsh. Subsequently, however, the Portuguese obtained a new liberal constitution in 1822.

▼ *The Douro River and the city after sunset*

Port, king of wines

King of all the wines of Portugal is undoubtedly the legendary Port, produced in the region of the Douro, matured – by law – in the lodges in the zone of Vila Nova de Gaia nearby. There are different kinds – as will be explained further on – but whichever one you choose, the wine must always be poured from a pitcher. It was apparently first created in the early 1900s, thanks to the agronomic-commercial collaboration between the English and the Portuguese, and is now one of the finest wines in the world and exported to all continents, thanks also to the characteristics of the vines which produce it, with roots that go down into the earth as deep as twelve meters. The authoritative Instituto do Vinho do Porto (Port Wine Institute) supervises the vineyards in the Alto Douro area, where there are various types of grapes, and rigorously controls every step in the long process required before the wine ends up on some lucky table. Grown under the supervision of expert agronomists in the numerous Quintas, large and enchanting white farms or estates, after its fermentation it is taken to Vila Nova de Gaia in barrels where it remains for years to mature. Every bottle, at the end, must bear the selo de origem, a distinctive mark which testifies to its origin and quality. At the vertex of Port is the so-called vintage Port, as famous as it is expensive, obtained from grapes of a single vintage year defined by the experts as a golden year. For example 1963, 1977, 1985 were golden years. Years are required for its maturation and it is considered excellent after ten, but supreme after fifteen or twenty years. Another equally famous but not quite as exclusive quality is "Port with delayed bottling". One more in this list is the so-called "Port matured in wood", the result of a mixture of different vintage years matured in oak casks. So much has been written about Port, as about all legendary wines,

▼ A splendid picture of the Douro Valley

endowed with a rich symbolism and precise rituals, which includes tasting, which the traveler can learn by visiting the areas of production in Portugal and the great wine lodges.

Among the best known types of Port are the Blendel, white or red, Vintage, matured in the bottle as well, LVB (Late-Bottled Vintage wine), port wine from a single vintage. Outstanding also the Ruby, a dessert port and the Tawny, with long maturing time.

But Port is not the only Portuguese wine. The country produces many other excellent wines including the well known and appreciated vinhos verdes, which come from the zone of Minho, south-western territory of Portugal. Vine growing has ancient traditions here and employs almost two hundred thousand people. Vinho verde can be white (branco) or red (tinto), and is a light slightly sparkling wine of never more than eleven percent alcoholic content and will vary according to the six zones of origin and production. This wine too – grown in pergolas and not in rows - is protected and guaranteed by an "Association of producers and bottlers of vinho verde".

Good Portuguese wines also come from various other regions such as Bairrada, near Coimbra, which makes an excellent red, or Douro itself which produces other wines in addition to the famous Port.

▲ Reaper on an azulejo in the station of Pinhão

▲ The vineyards of the Douro Valley

◄ The "Vinho", detail of a commercial azulejo in the Mercado do Bolhão in Oporto

▲ Praça da Liberdade

ordained bishop by Saint Peter and was a friend and close collaborator of Saint Paul. In the year 96 he helped write the first *Letter to the Church of Corinth*. The Igreja dos Congregados also has the tombs of two other popes: São Silverio, or Saint Silverius, elected pope in 536 during the period of Justinian, and Saint Eugenius I, pope from 654 to 657.

Next comes a walk in *Rua de Santa Catarina*, a fashionable pedestrian street for shopping, where elegant boutiques have sprung up side by side with the

▼ *Igreja dos Congregado the facade decorated with azulej*

The Baixa is the center, the heart, of the lower city which winds along around the *Avenida dos Aliados* (of the Allies), a broad two-lane tree-shaded avenue with a walkway at the center with benches and gardens, closed on the north by the **Paço do Concelho**, the town hall, with a tower, and on the south by the **Praça da Liberdade**, where all the streets leading to the different districts flow together. The equestrian statue of king Pedro IV rises up over the crowded square. At the corner of the square is the **Igreja dos Congregados** dedicated to Saint Anthony. The sober facade is decorated with azulejos. Inside a fine *pulpit* and a *retable in talha dourada* are in the side **Chapel** of the **Sagrada Família**. Beneath the altar is the tomb of Saint Clement I, martyr and pope from 88 to 97, the fourth after Saint Peter. He was

Rua de Santa Catarina and, ▲ the foreground, Art Nouveau reliefs

▲ Azulejo with floral decoration

▲ The Mercado do Bolhão

old dusty shops where garden seeds, wine and dried salted cod are sold. A required ritual is that of sitting at one of the oldest cafés in the city, the **Majestic**, where waiters in livery serve pastries, tea, coffee and a few main dishes at wood and marble tables. In the parallel *Rua Sá da Bandeira* – across from the old typical shop selling coffee, tea and cocoa *A Pérola do Bolhão* all in wood and azulejos – inside an im-

posing metal structure is the large noisy *Mercado do Bolhão*, full of joyous Portuguese in the midst of fresh fish, vegetables, meet, cheese and fruit. To the north, in the neighboring **Praça da Batalha**, at the top of the hill, is the **Igreja de Santo Ildefonso** with an imposing staircase. The facade with its two towers is faced in blue and white azulejos which narrate the *Life of the Saint*.

◄ The old Café Majestic in Rua de Santa Catarina

▼ The typical coffee shop A Pérola do Bolhão

▼ Torre dos Clérigos,
symbol of the city,
by Nicola Nasoni

▲ *Igreja dos Clérigos, the oval interi*

In nearby **Cordoaria** – the district of parks and gardens like **São Lázaro** with its palms, cedars and cypresses, the haunt of the students of the neighboring university, full of restaurants and shops, steep streets and clanking trams – is the monument symbol of the city, the **Torre dos Clérigos**. This stone tower with its clock has been the point of reference and of arrival for sailors for centuries.

Climbing the two hundred and twenty-five steps to the top of the six story, seventy-six meter high Tower provides a splendid vista over the city, the river and the Ocean. The Baroque tower is one of the most important works by the Italian architect Nicola Nasoni, as is the original **Igreja dos Clérigos**. Built between 1735 and 1748, its elegant architecture makes it one of the most beautiful churches in the city. The facade is richly decorated and the interior is oval in plan.

Continuing our walk in **Praça Gomes Teixeira**, with the lion fountain and palms, the Igreja do Carmo and the Igreja dos Carmelitas stand next to each other. They say that the latter is the church of the poor and for the poor, open at any time of day and always crowded. Built around 1600, it has a fine altar decorated

Igreja do Carmo, its wall lined with azulejos

in *talha dourada* and two elegant *pulpits* in gilded stone. The sumptuous **Igreja do Carmo** on the other hand was built in the eighteenth century by José Figueiredo Seixas. The outer wall is faced with azulejos by master Silvestro Silvestri and narrate the *Story of the Carmelites*. The facade has three levels and many statues. The single nave interior glitters with gold on the columns and altars. A frescoed dome stands over the high altar.

In the *Rua dos Carmelitas*, behind the church of the same name, is the **Livraria Lello**, an Art Nouveau bookstore, an institution in Oporto and which has been the sacred temple of books since 1881. These include antique books, all in a setting of polychrome stained glass windows, staircases, balustrades and galleries in wood, with the sculptured heads of the Portuguese men of letters.

▶ *Casa Oriental, historical shop of colonial products in the Cordoaria*

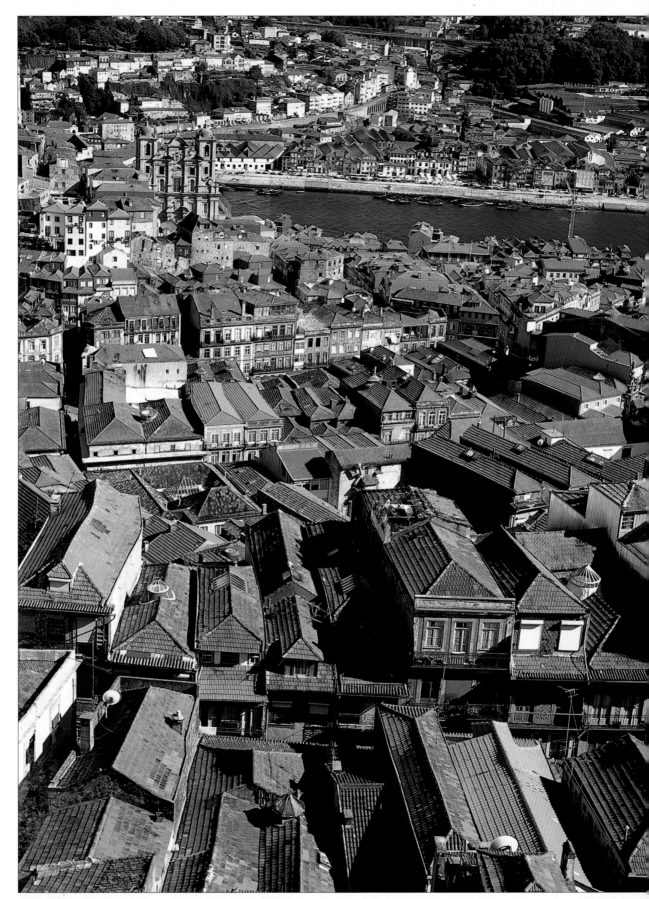

▲ *Panorama of the city from the Torre dos Clérigos*

Bairro da Sé

▶ *The Pelourinho,
the penitential column on the Terreiro da Sé*

The cathedral stands on the top of the Pena Ventosa hill and overlooks the entire district and its monuments and historical buildings. It is from here that the upper city is best seen, while below lie the Barredo district and the others, less luxurious, which lead to the river. A **Pelourinho**, or *penitential column*, in Manueline style, twisted with rostra and a wreath at the top, set on the **Terreiro da Sé**, embodies municipal authority.

The Romanesque cathedral, with the **Paço Episcopal** on its right, is imposing and massive, rather like a fortress, and still has the crenellated bartizan

View of the Cathedral and its district

▲ *The imposing Sé Catedral*

where the soldiers once kept watch. It was built in the twelfth century on a Suebian construction, when the city was already an archbishop's see, but much of its original style was lost in the course of restorations and enlargements. The facade has a fine Romanesque *rose window* in the center, with the image of *God the Father*, and a finely wrought *portal*. Square bell towers stand on either side while an elegant loggia in granite decorated with azulejos by the Italian architect Nicola Nasoni is on the side facade. It dates to 1736 and is a sensitive union of harmony and proportion. The interior has a nave separated from the two aisles by powerful piers and side chapels. In the chapel to the left of the entrance is a bronze *Baptism of Christ* by

► Sé, the baptismal font by Teixeira Lopes the Elder

Sé, the loggia on the side entrance, by Nicola Nasoni

Teixiera Lopes the Elder. The solid silver seventeenth century altar in the **Capela do Santíssimo Sacramento** in the left transept is superb. Also worthy of note is the panel in gilded wood of *Christ at the Last Supper*, a seventeenth century work in the **Capela de São Vicente**. The two side loggias above the high altar were frescoed by Nasoni who tried his hand at painting here. They are unfortunately deteriorating and should be restored. The larger Gothic **Cloister** has two original thirteenth century arcades and azulejos panels on the walls illustrating the *Song of Songs*, while others represent scenes from Ovid's *Metamorphoses*. Chronicles say that it was here in this cathe-

▲ *Sé, Capela do Santíssimo Sacramento*

▼ *Sé, the richly decorated Gothic cloister with the towers*

dral that Philippa, the daughter of the count of Lancaster, and King João I, future parents of Henry the Navigator, were married in a sumptuous ceremony in 1387.

Behind the cathedral, in *Rua de D. Hugo*, is the municipal museum **Guerra Junqueiro**, a Baroque house of the eighteenth century which belonged to the writer Manuel de Guerra Junqueiro (1850-1923). The building, attributed to Nicola Nasoni, contains collections of goldwork, sculpture, ceramics, splendid examples of furniture in fine woods and Flemish tapestries. A hundred meters from the Sé, within the **Fernandine Walls**, built in the fourteenth century by Fernando I, is the **Igreja de Santa Clara** which was part of the convent of the Poor Clares found by order of the king in 1416. The

◄ *Sé, detail of the cloister with azulejos panels*

▲ *Sé, the small Moorish cloister and, in the foreground, a few tombs of the same period*

▼ *Azulejos panel with mythological scenes on the upper arcade of the cloister*

▲ View of the Port and the Fernandine walls

sober almost humble facade does not prepare one for the glittering golden interior. The church is a jewel, more harmonious than the church of São Francisco. Renovated several times, it has a Manueline Gothic *portal* of the sixteenth century. The single nave interior is entirely lined in *talha dourada*. The **Upper Choir** or church gallery with its splendid paintings and sculpture in *talha dourada* is outstanding. Here the nuns participated in the mass from behind grilles. From *Avenida Dom Afonso Henriques* along **Praça Almeida Garrett** one encounters the curious nineteenth century **Estação de São Bento**, the station built on the site of a Benedictine convent, with the entrance decorated in azulejo panels with scenes of the Portuguese conquests of the early 1900s by master Jorge Colaço.

▼ *Igreja de Santa Clara* the Manueline Gothic port*

▼ Detail of the Fernandine walls

◀▼ *Igreja de Santa Clara,*
the sumptuous high altar
in talha dourada and a putto,
detail of a side chapel

symbol of the Casa da Misericórdia created in 1499. This royal institution was founded by King Manuel I with a program of social works and assistance entrusted to lay personnel. The **Igreja da Misericórdia** was built in 1550 and restored in the eighteenth century. The facade was rebuilt to a design by Nasoni and has Rococo influences and is decorated with statues. The interior is still extraordinarily sober.

From the square walk along *Rua das Flores,* the street of flowers, citadel of jewelers, gold and silversmiths, with elegant middle-class dwellings, narrow long buildings, some with tiles and wrought iron windows and balconies. At the beginning is the **Igreja** and **Museu de Santa Casa da Misericórdia**. The museum has been installed in a metal structure and its wealth of precious objects, sacred art and numerous paintings includes a splendid sixteenth century *Annunciation* by Teixeira Lopes and a famous sixteenth century painting, the *Fons Vitae,* of Flemish school but uncertain attribution (Holbein and Van Dyck). This painting shows the *crucified Christ,* his blood flowing into a fountain supported by King Manuel I and his family. It is the

▶ *Art Nouveau goldsmith's shop in Rua Trindade Coelho*

▲ *Museu de Santa Casa da Misericórdia,*
view of the interior

▲ *Museu de Santa Casa da Misericórdia,*
finely decorated solid gold chalice

▲ *Museu de Santa Casa da Misericórdia,*
Annunciation by Teixeira Lopes

▶ *Museu de Santa Casa da Misericórdia,*
the famous painting of the Fons Vitae

The Ribeira

The *Rua Escura* – the name, dark street, itself tells you much – below the cathedral near the noisy market with its umbrella-covered stands of fruit, vegetables, fresh fish and a host of knickknacks and souvenirs, takes us into the narrow lanes which seem so close they almost touch each other in the **Barredo**, **Miragaia**, **Ribeira** districts which move down towards the river like a funnel. Here in this densely packed site is the true soul of Oporto, made of misery, nobility and *Saudade*, the smell of fried food, roasted sardines and humidity, with women calling each other, children shouting, laundry hung out the windows of the tall narrow houses with chipped azulejos or painted in all tones of ocher yellow and Pompeii red. Countless birds and gulls wheel overhead. This is a magic place, the most sublime of Oporto, full of life and charm where tourists, young

▲ *The Rua Escura leading to the Ribeira*

Typical colored houses along the Douro River

▲ *The Cais da Ribeira from the Dom Luís I Bridge*

people, lovers, businessmen meet in the many small restaurants, fried-food shops, *adegas*, and taverns (greasy spoons) along the Cais da Ribeira up to the **Praça da Ribeira**, the center of the district, ending up the evening in the wine cellars of Vila Nova de Gaia, across the *Dom Luís I Bridge*. Alongside the Cais is a picturesque market of pedlars and stands, selling wares ranging from food to pottery, lupins and bird seed, and fuzzy woolen sweaters every day of the week including Sundays. This is where one can buy the good Portuguese olives and an exquisite brown bread to be found only here, with a thick crisp crust, the *broa de milho* made with hard wheat and maize. Speaking of food this is also the place to discover why the Portuguese *bacalhau* is not stringy but particularly soft: the secret is that it is cooked in milk.

In *Rua do Cimo do Muro da Ribeira* there is an *Elevador* that runs through a tunnel two meters wide,

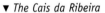

▼ *The Cais da Ribeira*

◄ *The Ribeira and, above, the Paço Episcopal*

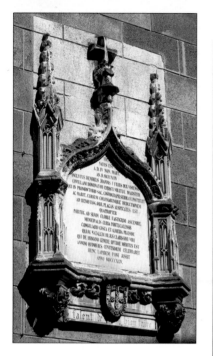

◄ *Casa do Infante Dom Enrique the Navigator, commemorative plaque*

► *Rua de Miragaia*

dug out in a house, which for a few escudos takes one to a terrace with a marvelous view over the red roofs of the Ribeira, Barredo, Lada districts and the Fernandine walls. Coming down from the *Arco da Ribeira* in *Rua dos Canastreiros* and then towards *Rua da Alfândega*, the customs street in the Miragaia district, one encounters the **Casa do Infante Dom Henrique the Navigator**, now seat of the Historical Archives. During restoration work, Roman mosaics and remains were discovered in the house.

A vast reclamation program is in course in the Ribeira, under the auspices of Unesco since 1996. The district in itself is a medieval monument, but there are a few other things that should be seen, such as the **Igreja de São Francisco**, a triumph of Baroque and *talha dourada*. The Franciscan church was built in the fourteenth century, but subsequently was altered and restored more than once. The fine *rose window* belongs to the original Gothic structure, while the nave and two aisles of the interior are an elaborate glittering gold embroidery. The ceiling, the altars, the pillars, the choir, the figures, animals and angels, are all gilded. It is said that two hun-

◄ *Igreja de São Francisco*

To the left of the church, in *Rua Ferreira Borges*, the street of the **Instituto do Vinho do Porto** on the site of the old Franciscan convent, the merchants, at the time members of the *Associação Comercial do Porto*, in 1842 financed the construction of the **Bolsa**, the Stock Market building. It is a fine Neoclassic structure designed by the architect Joaquim da Costa Lima. One of the finest and most scenic rooms is the oval **Salão Árabe** or Arabian Hall, of obvious Moorish influence. The walls and the ceiling are decorated with Arabesque stuccoes and friezes, covered in gold leaf. The artisan, Gonçalves de Sousa, used eighteen kilograms of gold in the execution. When the lights are turned on in this room which recalls the Spanish Alhambra the glitter is blinding.

▲▶ *Igreja de São Francisco, the interior, a triumph of Baroque, and decorations in talha dourada in a side chapel*

dred kilograms of gold were used for the gilding at a moment when Portugal was at the height of its economic power.

Of particular note in the midst of all this glitter is a thirteenth century polychrome granite statue of *Saint Francis*, the poor friar, in a corner. In the second side chapel is a sculpture in *talha dourada* of the *Tree of Jesse*, the biblical genealogical tree with Isaiah, David, Solomon up to the Holy Family. Inside the church, no longer consecrated, the **crypt** contains an ossuary and a small museum of sacred art as well as the elegant tomb of a wealthy sixteenth century merchant, Francisco Brandão Pereira.

◀ Igreja de São Francisco, the Tree of Jesse

▲ The Salão Árabe in the Palácio da Bo

◀ The Mercado Ferreira Borges

Boavista

This is the suburb, north of the city, with new houses. The main street is *Avenida da Boavista*, full of hotels, banks, shops and a large mall, the largest in the city. At the center of the Avenida the **Praça de Mouzinho de Albuquerque**, more familiarly known as the *Rotunda*, with the allegorical sculpture of a lion astride over a rather flattened eagle, symbol of the Anglo-Portuguese victory over Napoleon. In addition to a Synagogue, this district has the eleventh century **Igreja de Cedofeita**, a fine example of early Romanesque. It is the oldest church in the city and has unfortunately changed considerably, the last renovation dating to the eighteenth century. It was built on the site of an earlier sixth century church after the Suevian king Theodomir was converted to Christianity by Saint Martin. Indeed the name *Cedo Feita* means "in all haste". The church with a nave only is open only Saturdays and Sundays. It is almost bare and has a high altar which dates to 1087 while the *portal* with columns and animal capitals is Romanesque.

▲ *The eleventh century Igreja de Cedofeita*

▼ *A typical wrought iron window in a house in Foz do Douro*

Foz do Douro

Foz do Douro, or São João da Foz, is the light-filled district at the mouth of the Douro River, on the Ocean. In the early 1900s it was still a fishing hamlet and vacation site. Now it is part of the city with fine beaches, well cared-for palm lined avenues, flourishing gardens, luxury dwellings and mansions. It is the district of the wealthy middle-class entrepreneurs. The district is dominated by a **lighthouse** and the **Castelo do Queijo** dating to 1570.

New life has been given to the neighboring plain industrial center of **Matosinhos** by the futuristic buildings of the contemporary architect Álvaro Siza Vieira and the artificial port of **Leixões**. Of particular note is a *wooden Christ* in the eighteenth century Baroque church, the **Bom Jesus**, rebuilt by Nicola Nasoni. In the *Romaria*, the festival celebrated in the month of June, pilgrims flock in from all parts to pay their devoted respects to the Christ of Matosinhos. Traditionally the statue of this venerated Jesus was found in the tenth century on the beach and is said to date to the year 50 and to have been carved by a follower of Nicodemus, the Judean notable who brought the unguents to embalm the body of Jesus Christ.

 ▲ *The oceanside promenade of Foz do Douro*

▲ Foz do Douro, the Castelo do Queijo

▶ Foz do Douro, the pier with the lighthouse

◀ Matosinhos, the artificial port of Leixões

▶ Matosinhos, Igreja de Bom Jesus de Boucas

Museums of Oporto

▲ Museu do Carro Eléctrico, the historical tram No. 18

Museu Romântico, Museu de Arte Moderna, Museu do Carro Eléctrico, Museu de Etnografia e História – these are the museums of Oporto. The most important is unquestionably the **Museu Nacional Soares dos Reis**, named after the Portuguese sculptor Soares dos Reis. It houses some of the most beautiful, important, and above all varied collections of art, ranging from ceramics to archaeological finds, paintings such as the splendid picture of the Virgem do Leite (Virgin suckling the Christ Child) by Carlos Frei.

Some of the rooms are used for temporary exhibitions of Portuguese artists.

The museum contains the most important examples of painting of the various schools: Academic, Romantic, Naturalistic, and paintings by artists such as Silva Porto and the Marquês de Oliveira, as well as sculpture. Of particular note is the superb sculpture O Desterrado (The Exile) by Soares dos Reis in a classic style which embodies both plastic tension and melancholy, and works by Teixeira Lopes such as the Infância de Caim. There are also collections of paintings of Flemish, French and Italian paintings.

Be sure to see the splendid silver bust of the patron saint of Oporto, São Pantaleão, and the sword that belonged to the first king of Portugal Afonso Henriques.

▼ Museu Soares dos Reis, detail of a Namban screen (Japan, seventeenth century)

Of particular interest in the **Museu Romântico** are the objects in the apartments where King Charles Albert of Savoy lived briefly after his abdication. Elegant French, German and Portuguese furniture, as well as carpets, ceramics and paintings. The portraits of Baron Forrester and Almeida Garrett are magnificent.

The **Museu de Arte Moderna** is an elegant villa, in a rationalist style, of the 1930s. With its magnificent gardens it is the most extensive green area inside Oporto. It contains one of the finest collections of modern art in the country.

Singular and eccentric is the **Museu do Carro Eléctrico**, installed in an old tram shed, where dozens of old restored trams are housed ranging from one drawn by mules to the first electric tram in the Iberian peninsula.

One can also take a ride on the historical tram number 18 which goes from the museum to the Boavista district, and the fare is rather inexpensive.

In ending our interesting round of Oporto and its museums, we must not forget the **Museu de Etnografia e História**, in a splendid eighteenth-century palace built by the Italian architect Nicola Nasoni. The usages and customs of the Valle del Douro are illustrated here, as well as bucolic scenes and, strangely enough, the first elevator of the city of Oporto dating to 1910.

▶ Museu Soares dos Reis, O Desterrado (The Exile) by Soares dos Reis

▲ *The wine lodges on the left bank of the Douro River and the Barcos Rabelos*

VILA NOVA DE GAIA

Vila Nova de Gaia is the suburb city, on the other side of the Dom Luís I Bridge, and it is the sacred place of *vinho do Porto*, where the *armazéns*, the wine lodges perched between the hill and the river, are to be found, and where the wine is matured in accordance with the law.

Gigantic letters on their roofs declare the name of the lodge: Sandeman, Cálem, Ferreira Pinto. Only about fifteen of the around sixty wine lodges can be visited to taste the excellent vintage Port.

The monument that dominates the town from the top of the hill is the Augustinian **Monastery of Serra do Pilar**. Built by the Italian architect Filippo Terzi (1520-1597), it is now used by the army. Only the church, open on Sundays, can be visited. The church has a circular ground plan and a splendid dome. Thirty-six Ionic columns decorate the cloister, which is also circular. The square in front of the church is one of the finest *miradouro* in the city, with splendid views over Vila Nova de Gaia and Oporto.

The fishermen's district, *Afurada*, has houses plastered white, a small church and laundry hung every-

▲ *The wine lodges of the Vinho do Porto*

where to dry. There is a small but interesting **Museu Teixeira Lopes** and **Galeria Diogo de Macedo** in Vila Nova de Gaia with a collection of sculptures by Teixeira Lopes, African art and paintings by the artist Diogo de Macedo.

▼ *Mosteiro da Serra do Pilar*

The Rabelos

That small fleet of "barcos rabelos" at anchor on the Douro, in front of Vila Nova de Gaia, is the symbol of Oporto and its vinho, *called sweet nectar. The* Rabelos *are special boats, apparently fragile, long, with a flat bottom, designed to transport barrels, with their square sails on which the names of the wine lodges are written: Sandeman, Ferreira Pinto, Cálem, Taylor.*

The wine produced in the golden triangle of the valley of the Upper Douro was transported on the Rabelos *in barrels up to the lodges in Vila Nova de Gaia where it would be matured. Their flat bottoms were ideal for navigating the treacherous river with its rapids. When moving upstream or with shallow water they were pulled by oxen. The* barcos, *built in*

▲ *Rabelo boats with Cais da Ribeira in the background*

▲▼ *Transporting barrels of wine, on an azulejo in the station of Pinhão and a brightly colored Rabelo boat with barrels*

pine, twenty-five meters long and six meters wide, have sails that are eighty meters square and they could transport sixty barrels containing five hundred twenty liters of wine each.

They say that the Rabelo *is of Viking origins and its elongated shape recalls the ships of that great people of navigators who around the tenth century sailed along the coasts of the Portuguese waters towards the Mediterranean. Nowadays the* Rabelos *are much more prosaically used simply as a tourist attraction.*

The Douro now runs calm, regulated by five dams (barragens). *The railroad has been developed and new roads have been built. Wine is now transported by heavy trucks. Even so a date to keep track of is the regatta of the* Rabelos *on June 24 for the feast of Saint John. The boats, representing the various wine lodges, leave from the mouth of the Douro and sail up to the Dom Luís I Bridge.*

VILA DO CONDE

▲ *Little girls of the Escola Museu de Rendas (Lace-making School)*

Vila do Conde, the city of the count, is a busy pleasure-loving provincial town with naval construction yards for fishing boats, industries for the processing of African and South American cotton, and a well-developed craft industry which the city puts on show in the annual **Feira de Artesanato** in the first week of August. Vila do Conde is famous throughout the world also for its pillow lace. This tradition and passion, which has been going on for over a thousand five hundred years, is shared by Viana do Castelo. The laces are real masterpieces made by skilful hands and the secrets of the trade are handed down from mother to daughter. Since the early 1900s the technique of this sublime art of making lace has also been taught to little girls from the age of four and up in the **Escola Museu de Rendas**, in *Rua de São Bento*. In the show cases here precious elaborate laces are to be seen. One in particular is of unique beauty and it is said it took more

▼ *The splendid beach with the city in the background*

▲ *The shop of a tinker*

bonfires on the beach, waiting for the *madrugada* – dawn.

The imposing **Mosteiro de Santa Clara**, almost a fortress near the river, overlooks the city. Founded in 1318 but subsequently modified and enlarged, the church and the fine cloister are open to the public. The Monastery, which was transformed into a prison from 1902 to 1944, now houses a boarding school for boys with social problems. Some of them accompany the tourists when they come.

The **Church**, with a baroque facade, houses the richly decorated stone tombs of the founder of the entire complex Dom Afonso Sanches and his numerous family in the **Capela da Conceição**. The **Sacristy** contains the portraits of the nuns who lived there until 1834, when the religious orders in Portugal were abolished.

In the fine eighteenth century **Cloister** there is a fountain where the **Aqueduct**, once near the Monastery and now in ruins, ended in the eighteenth century. It was five kilometers long with nine hundred ninety arches, and its water came from the neighboring town of Póvoa de Varzim.

than two years to make it and one thousand four hundred lace pillows. Laces of all types, and for all pocketbooks, can be bought in the school shop while in the **Centro de Artesanato** (Rua 5 de Outubro), where one can buy everything, it is usual to encounter old women seated and making pillow lace, swiftly interlacing the spindles to create splendid lace collars and shawls.

Vila do Conde with its twenty-three thousand inhabitants is located at the mouth of the Ave River, and while in winter it is a peaceful city, in summer it is overrun by vacation tourism which crowds the lovely beaches with their fine sand, **Praia da Forno** and **Praia de Nossa Senhora da Guia**, to bursting. But nothing can compare to the summer solstice celebration of Saint John, when the entire city is illuminated by candles and a long fascinating processions winds its way through. The streets later become dance floors, where the crowd eats, drinks and dances in the midst of fireworks and

▶ *A woman embroidering in her workshop*

▲ *Mosteiro de Santa Clara, the imposing eighteenth century facade*

The heart of the old city is in the small **Praça Vasco da Gama**, with a sixteenth century **Pelourinho**, or *penitential column,* at the center and the **Igreja Matriz**. This lovely little parish church was built in 1500 in the Manueline style with an original Plateresque portal (the *plateros* were the Spanish silversmiths) carved by the great Basque artist João de Castilho. On the pediment is the statue of *Saint John* and the symbols of the four evangelists, while inside the church is an interesting sixteenth century *pulpit* in *talha dourada.*

To the south, only three kilometers from Vila do Conde, on the right bank of the Ave River, is **Azurara**, a delightful fishermen's village with a small port,

a fine beach and a sixteenth century Manueline church. The restaurants along the ocean boulevard offer the best *caramelo leite-creme* in all of Portugal as well as cuisine based on fish.

► *Mosteiro de Santa Clara, the eighteenth century cloister with the fountain at the center*

► *The Igreja Matriz with its original Plateresque portal*

▲ *Eighteenth century aqueduct and the Igreja de São Francisco behind the arches*

▼ *Igreja Matriz, interior*

PÓVOA DE VARZIM

▲ *The monument dedicated to the women of the sea, in the area of the port*

Póvoa de Varzim, on the Atlantic Ocean, near Vila do Conde, is another vacation and fishing town, with an old port. The *Bairro*, the fishermen's district, south of the sandy beach and reefs, is characterized by the low houses that line the pretty bay.

The town is well equipped with residential buildings, hotels, pensions, discothèques, restaurants and coffee bars on the ocean boulevards. There are also tennis courts, a casino and the **Praça de Touros** where the Lusitanian *touradas* take place.

This is the favorite seaside resort for Portuguese from the North and unfortunately the building rules have not always been respected.

▲ *Fishing boats in the port of Póvoa*

Fortress of Nossa Senhora da Conceição

Póvoa de Varzim, which was a Roman colony, is where the novelist Eça de Queiroz (1845-1900) was born and has dedicated a monument to him in front of the **Paço do Concelho**. The city also has what remains of an eighteenth century **Fortress** and the parish **Church**.

▼ *View of the beach*

▲ *Viana do Castelo, at the mouth of the Lima River and a stretch of the Costa Verde*

▲ Ferryboats on the Lima River

VIANA DO CASTELO

Viana do Castelo is a charming city in the Minho region, lying softly on the estuary of the Lima River in the green valley at the base of Mount Santa Luzia. All the streets and lanes lead to this azure river. It is a famous resort on the Costa Verde of the Atlantic, with fine sandy beaches. The city, known as the capital of folklore, has a wealth of signs of its past and its naval construction yards are among the most important in Portugal. It has a deep-sea fishing port and a flourishing craft activity, both of which are at the basis of its economy.

Viana d Castelo, which has always been a bishop's see, is a deeply religious city, as is all of northern Lusitania. The North has the finest *Romarias*, religious celebrations dedicated to the patron saint which, with the passing of centuries, are not as severe as they once were, although they are still truly

▲ *Typical hand-made pottery and fine embroidery in Viana do Castelo*

religious celebrations despite the addition of fairs, folklore and gastronomy. A folk *Romaria* which is particularly moving and in which many participate is the **Festa de Nossa Senhora da Agonia,** Our Lady of Suffering, celebrated for three days in the third week of August. The streets are then sprinkled with large-grain salt or colored sawdust, instead of the costly rose petals of yore, where the procession will pass, with the Virgin under a baldachin carried by the men, almost always fishermen. The procession then continues in the sea, on the fishing boats. After the liturgical celebrations, the city goes wild with bands playing, dances in traditional folk costumes and parades of floats. Visitors then stuff themselves with *assada de peixe* (roast fish) and the *torta de Viana* made with flour, sugar and eggs. Wine flows in rivers. The celebration ends with fireworks on the river, a bull fight, the *tourada*, and the blessing of the fishing boats.

The origins of Viana do Castelo go far back, to the iron age, when it was a Celtiberian *Citânia*, the remains of which can be seen on the hill of Santa Luzia. It then became Roman and was known as Diana and its splendid river seduced the new conquerors. Tradition says that they thought of the Lima River as the mythological Lethe which cancelled memory and therefore avoided crossing it.

Viana do Castelo did not become a real city until 1258 with Afonso III who gave it a statute and a port at the mouth of the river. The importance of the har-

► *Typical decoration done with colored sawdust for the Festa de Nossa Senhora da Agonia*

▲ *The Procession in the Sea of Nossa Senhora da Agonia*

◄▼ *Folklore costumes worn*
for the Festa de Nossa Senhora da Agonia

▲ *Praça da República,*
heart of the historical center

of neighboring Spain, and with João V the city achieved its zenith thanks to the gold and diamonds which arrived from Brazil. In the eighteenth century the English merchants who had established themselves in the city and traded in textiles began to appreciate and send the good local wine to England. They called it "Portuguese red". Thus began the fortunes of the *Vinho do Porto* and the city of Oporto, while Viana do Castelo slowly began to decline.

The **Praça da República** is the heart of the historical center, the splendid parlor of the

bor grew in the sixteenth century and it was from here that the caravels weighed anchor and went to discover far-distant worlds, returning loaded with merchandise. The cod fishermen left from here for the waters of Newfoundland which the Portuguese had just discovered (1500). And the *conquistador* João Velho left from here for Africa. So much money flowed in from the new conquests that the city became an enormous construction yard, and monasteries, monuments, churches and palaces were built. Viana do Castelo became a sea port which dealt with far-off countries and hosted people from all over the world. Under King João II the city opened its doors to a large community of Jews who had just been driven out

▶ *Casa da Misericórdia,*
by the Portuguese architect
João Lopes the Younger

Igreja Matriz, Gothic sculpture decorating the portal

João Lopes the Younger, has a facade with two loggias supported by twelve elegant caryatids. Next to it, the **Igreja da Misericórdia**, entirely rebuilt in 1714, has splendid white and blue azulejo panels inside, a sumptuous altar in *talha dourada* and side chapels in polychrome marbles and gilded intarsia.

The parish church, **Igreja Matriz**, built in 1400 and restored more than once, is the other monument near the square. The facade with two Romanesque towers still has a splendid imposing Gothic portal decorated with statues of the figures of Christ and the Apostles and with a rose window further up. The interior of the church is decorated with azulejos and paintings, while the lovely *Baptism of Jesus* is in *talha dourada*.

The **Museu Municipal** of Viana do Castelo is housed in the fine **Palácio Barbosa Maciel** in *Largo de São Domingos* where there is a church of the same name.

city, considered the most beautiful square in the Minho region and where the most important sixteenth century monuments are located. The **Castelo de São Tiago da Barra** dating to the eighteenth century lies at the mouth of the river and overlooks the picturesque fishermen's district. The square has a Renaissance fountain by João Lopes the Elder dating to 1554. The **Paços do Conçelho** stands proud on the square. The old sixteenth century building is a solid construction, in stone with Gothic arches and windows and Manueline decoration. The **Casa da Misericórdia**, also a Renaissance building by the Portuguese architect

▶ *Igreja Matriz with its twin towers*

▲ Igreja da Misericórdia, the interior with the altar in talha dourada and splendid azulejos panels

◀ Palácio de Carreira

▼ Museu Municipal
fine pieces of furniture inlaid in ivory

Museu Municipal, the extraordinary collection of Portuguese azulejos

▼ *The Capela de Nossa Senhora da Agonia, point of departure for the Romaria*

The museum is well worth visiting for it contains an extraordinary collection of a thousand six hundred pieces of ceramics, azulejo tiles from all over Portugal, precious Indo-Portuguese furniture in fine woods and ivory intarsias, numerous paintings and archaeological pieces of great worth. The small **Igreja de São Domingos**, built in 1570, was part of the Dominican convent. Inside, in addition to the tomb of Frei Bartolomeu dos Mártires, the founder of the church, the visitor's attention is drawn to the precious and elaborate altar in *talha dourada* in the **Capela de Nossa Senhora do Rosário**. Art historians say it is the finest example of Baroque in all of Portugal. Towards *Rua de São Tiago*, in the fishermen's district, is the church and Baroque **Capela de Nossa Senhora da Agonia**, constantly visited by pilgrims, above all during the *Romaria*.

From **Monte de Santa Luzia** there is a splendid panorama of the city and the estuary of its

▲ *Remains of the Celtiberian Citân̄ on Monte de Santa Luzia (fourth century B. C*

▼ *Basílica de Santa Luzia on the mounta of the same nan*

▲ *The cable car that goes to the Basílica de Santa Luzia*

river. For those who like to walk, it takes not much more than twenty minutes from the center (three kilometers) in the midst of pines and acacias. Otherwise there is an easy and enjoyable cable car which takes you to the top of the hill, to the **Basílica de Santa Luzia**, an early twentieth century building in Byzantine style, dedicated to the Sacred Heart, rather like the shrine in Paris. A monumental flight of stairs leads into the interior with its nave and two aisles. Be sure to see the poorly preserved remains of the Celtiberian **Citânia** of the fourth century B.C., half hidden in the flourishing vegetation.

BARCELOS

Barcelos is the city of the miraculous rooster which according to legend crowed even though already roasted and saved the life of a poor Galician pilgrim accused of theft. It is the city of the great market-fair on Thursdays, which has been going on since the fifteenth century, and it is the city where the best superbly cooked pork is eaten.

The peaceful medieval and agricultural town of Barcelos is located on the right bank of the Cávado River crossed by a fourteenth century **Stone bridge** with five spans. Life all goes on in the immense square, almost an esplanade: **Campo da Feira** or **Campo da República**. This is where on Thursdays farmers, vendors, artisans sell everything imaginable, from

▲ *Coat of arms of the Counts of Barcelos and Braganza*

View of the stone bridge over the Cávado River with the medieval town in the background

▲ The Market in Campo da Feira with local craft wares

vegetables to animals, pottery painted with yellow dots (the characteristic *louça de Barcelos*) as well as wicker baskets and chairs, wooden objects and furniture, copper utensils and pots such as the *cataplana* and lace and embroidery. As is to be expected, the famous rooster with his red crest who has become the symbol of Portugal is to be found everywhere.

A great number of tourists are also attracted to Barcelos for the **Folklore Festival** – held on the last Sunday in July with a review of folk dances and songs, fireworks, and rivers of *Vinho do Porto* – and the **Festa das Cruzes**, the festival of the crosses, celebrated on May 3. This is a *Romaria* of great religious significance, and Barcelos is decorated with garlands and colored lights with flowers scattered everywhere along the streets and crosses fixed in the ground. An impressive procession which recalls the Passion of Christ begins at the Igreja do Bom Jesus da Cruz and winds through the streets of the city. Tradition says that the festival began with the vision of the Cross a cobbler had around the year 1500.

Barcelos already existed in the Iron age, after which the Romans built a settlement. It did not

▲ *Igreja do Bom Jesus da Cruz*

really develop until the Middle Ages when it became the capital of the county of Portucale and residence of the duke of Braganza.

The city center and the historical districts are on the slopes that move down to the river and Campo da República. On the northern part of the square is the **Igreja de Nossa Senhora do Terço**, once part of a Benedictine monastery.

The interior of the church is of note, with a profusion of eighteenth century azulejos that even extend to the coffered ceiling. They are by the master António de Oliveira Bernardes and narrate the *Life of Saint Benedict*. The carved and gilded Baroque *pulpit* should not be missed.

◀ *Igreja de Nossa Senhora do Terço, the interior lined with eighteenth century azulejos and the Baroque pulpit*

▲ *Archaeological area in the ruins of the Paço dos Duques de Bragança*

◄ *Torre de Menagem*

On the opposite side of the square is another church, the **Igreja do Bom Jesus da Cruz**. The Greek cross building dates to 1705 and the architect was João Antunes. A fine granite dome rises up over the central octagonal part, completely covered inside with azulejos. Next to the church is the **Torre de Menagem**, housing the tourist office and a shop of local crafts. The imposing building facing the tower is the hospital in the old **Convento da Misericórdia** dating to 1649.

What was once the sumptuous fifteenth century **Paço dos Duques de Bragança**, is now no more than a ruin with the sky as its roof. It was one of the casualties of the terrible earthquake of 1755 which also destroyed so much of Lisbon. The **Archaeological Museum** has been installed in the midst

▼ *Cruzeiro do Senhor do Galo, stone crucifix, symbol of the city, and the facade of the Igreja Matriz*

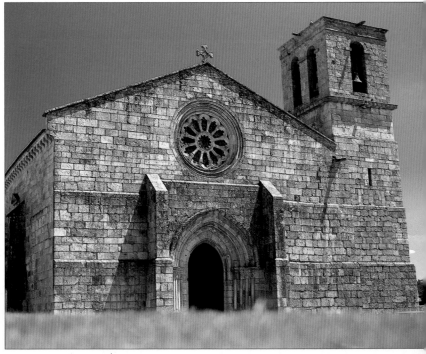

of these ruins. It contains a collection of Medieval granite objects and the famous fourteenth century stone *Crucifix* of the *Senhor do Galo*, traditionally carved by the Galician pilgrim in gratitude for having been saved. The **Museu da Cerâmica** is in one of the rooms under the palace. Next door is the Romanesque-Gothic parish church **Igreja Matriz**, with a splendid door and a rose window, while inside the eighteenth century blue and white azulejos on the walls are truly lovely. The side chapels are a riot of *talha dourada*.

The **Solar dos Pinheiros** is the Gothic noble palace across from the church. There is a curious sculpture on one of the towers, showing a man tearing his beard, the *Barbadão*. The other museum in the city, **Museu de Olaria**, has an ethnological collection of Lusitanian ceramics which present the history, technique, style and provenience of the tiles and this typically Portuguese art.

The Miraculous Rooster

*E*very tourist who returns from a trip to Portugal has one of the ubiquitous little roosters in his suitcase. The rooster is a symbol of Portugal and there is one in every Portuguese house or office.

The origins of this rooster symbol can be traced back to a miracle that seems to have taken place around the fifteenth century, when a tired and hungry pilgrim from Galicia who was on his way to the Shrine of Santiago de Compostela, stopped in the city of Barcelos. The next morning the pilgrim was accused of being a thief by a land owner and was condemned to death, despite his proclamations of innocence. He was taken before the judge who was at table about to eat a roast chicken. After explaining the situation, the pilgrim said that to show his innocence the roast chicken would begin crowing. And lo and behold, as the poor man was being taken to the gallows, the rooster stood up and began to crow. Thanks to that rooster the pilgrim's life was saved. In gratitude, years later he returned and carved a small rooster said to be the one now in the **Museu Arqueológico** of Barcelos.

CITÂNIA DE BRITEIROS

▲ *Panorama of the settleme*

The remains of a Celtiberian settlement from the Iron age (eighth to fourth cent. B.C.) are to be found on the hill of São Romão at Briteiros, between Guimarães and Braga.

The archaeological site was discovered in 1874 by the archaeologist Francisco Martins Sarmento and covers four hectares, with three circles of imposing walls and the foundations of a hundred and fifty houses with a circular ground plan. On the top of

▲ *Houses with circular floor plans*

the hill are a **Basilica** (recently built) and two perfectly restored **Houses**. One of the most significant and well preserved monuments of the entire settlement is the **Balneário**, a gigantic tomb. A map at the entrance to the site helps the tourist to identify the most interesting parts.

The city – inhabited by the Celtiberians, a warrior tribe of Iberians and Celts from whom the Lusitanians descend – was extremely well organized and was certainly their last fort before falling into the hands of the Romans.

Citânia had a truly ingenious irrigation system: the water which sprang from a spring in the hill passed through grooves dug out of the stone up to the cistern.

Many of the finds are in the **Museu de Martins Sarmento** in nearby Guimarães.

◄ *The Balneário, a gigantic well-preserved tomb*

BRAGA

Bracara Augusta, now known as Braga, lies in a plain, far from the sea. No river runs through this city, the capital of Minho, the greenest region of Portugal.

Clean and orderly, it is characterized by its flowers, colors, parks and fountains with their computerized jets and plays of water, to be found in every single square.

Braga is a profoundly religious tranquil city, marked by prayer and work. At nine in the evening the streets become deserted, shop signs go out, silence reigns, despite the growing number of tourists. For those who cannot sleep and for the tourists the gathering place is *Praça da República*. The long arcade, the **Arcada**, on this spacious lovely square has stands that stay open till late, and historical coffee houses such as the Café **Viana** and the elegant Café **Astória**, with wood paneling. During the day this is the realm of shoe-shine boys and vendors of tickets for the lottery, to which the Lusitanians are passionately devoted.

This is also the favorite rendezvous for students – ever since the founding of the **Universidade do Minho** in 1973. This Jesuit university with faculties of eco-nomics, theology, philosophy and literature, brought in a flood of young people from various countries, renewing and revitalizing a city that tended to be conservative and closed and with a population that was predominantly elderly.

The coup d'état which brought the dictator Oliveira de Salazar to power in 1926 began here in Braga.

Praça da República is the ideal place of departure for gastronomic raids, a place to become acquainted with the Minho cuisine, based on meat and easy to digest despite a generous use of butter. The most tempting dishes include *arroz de pato e chouriço* (rice prepared with duck and sausage), and broiled filet topped by a fried egg and lots of butter, with a side of grilled potatoes.

Braga, as we said, is a religious town. There is something to remind you of this fact wherever you turn, at whatever time of day beginning with the bells that toll on Sunday together with a carillon to announce the holy day and the beginning of the services, to the great number of religious shops in the historical center, side by side with fashion boutiques, where religious paraphernalia and holy images, wooden statues for household tabernacles, are sold. The num-

▼ *Praça da República*

▲ *Mile-marker columns in the old Roman Bracara Augusta*

ple, for its destiny was not and is not in the Ocean, was not and is not in the river and maritime trade. Yet it is thanks to this diversity that it has become rich, strong and powerful. As Portugal's religious capital, occasionally known as the "Lusitanian Rome" or the "Portuguese Vatican", Braga played an important role in building the immense Catholic colonial empire from which, on a geographical basis alone, it would have been excluded.

Braga was founded by the Bracarii, a Gallo-Celtic tribe who called it Bracara, before the Romans arrived in 250 B.C. and renamed it Bracara Augusta. At the time it was at the crossing of the five most important roads, and it rapidly developed. Around 410 A.D. the Suebi conquered the city and it became their capital until 585 A.D. Conquered by the Moors in 715, it fell to the Christians in 740 and then was once more Arab until 1040.When it became an Episcopal see in the twelfth century, buildings of note began to go up. It became the seat of the Primate of All Spain, a right the church retained for six centuries. The archbishops at that time became the lords of Braga and governed it until 1792. Still today the city is the most important center for religious studies in Portugal.

Walking is easy in Braga for there are no steep roads, and everything to see is in the historical center, approximately one kilometer square. Life in the city rotates around *Rua de D. Diogo de Sousa, Largo do Paço, Rua do Souto*, which is a pedestrian street with elegant shops, and then *Praça da República*, with parks, fountains and the **Torre de Menagem**, the fourteenth century keep. Any visit must begin with the most important monument in the city, the Sé Catedral.

ber of churches is also striking: there are forty-five, rich, opulent, Baroque, the prevailing style in Braga. Sunday mass and the daily reciting of the rosary are customary in Braga, as is the devotion for the saints and the Virgin Mary.

Traditions and holidays are particularly important here and are, at one and the same time, recreation and affirmation of the faith. An example are the *Romarias* or pilgrimage festivals and those dedicated to the patron saint or in those of the *Semana Santa*, Holy Week, when the Calvary of Christ is reenacted with deep felt participation and intensity. But whatever the celebration, it is always followed by an opulent banquet, folk dances and music.

Modern Braga has two hundred thousand inhabitants. Growth is in the suburbs with new residential quarters and any number of industries, not to mention the crafts, an important aspect in its economy.

But Braga is also the agrarian center, the bread-basket for all of Lusitania. Historically, anthropologically, traditionally, it is the land of those who till the soil, of farmers, rustic peo-

▶ *Gothic decorations on the Sé*

▲ *Sé Catedral, the west facade with the fifteenth century portico*

bronze tomb of the Infante Dom Afonso, son of João I. Philip, Bartholomew, James can be identified among the many statues of saints adorning the walls of the church. The **high altar** is a masterpiece of ivory carving and in front is a magnificent medieval statue of *Saint Mary of Braga*, the patron of the city, while the vaulting of the dome is in Flamboyant style, raying out in a great wheel. In the left transept is the **Capela de São Pedro de Rates**. The walls are covered with azulejos which narrate the *life* of this saint who was archbishop of Braga. The pair of organs, decorated in *talha dourada* with allegorical figures which also support the eighteenth century **Upper Choir** or church gallery with its superb wooden stalls gilded with Brazilian gold.

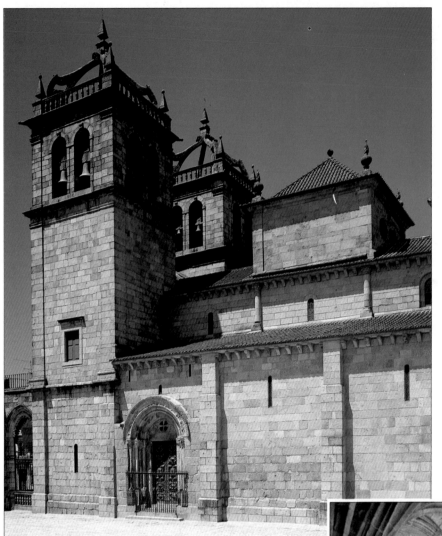

▲ *Sé Catedral, the south side*

▼ *Sé, the portic and the Gothic vaultin*

After its construction in the twelfth century, the **Sé Catedral** was renovated many times, restored and enlarged. Henry of Burgundy count of Portucale wanted this cathedral, an Episcopal seat, to be as imposing as possible, rivaling the famous Shrine of Santiago de Compostela, in the neighboring Galicia. The cathedral has a central body surrounded by chapels, and twin towers. The mixture of styles ranges from its original Romanesque to the Baroque, passing through Gothic, Renaissance and Manueline. The **Porta do Sol** (South Portal) and the **arches** over the central portal, later adorned with sculpture, are Romanesque. There is an extraordinary sixteenth century *Madonna Suckling the Christ Child* by Nicolas Chanterène in a niche. The Latin-cross church has a nave and two aisles. Upon entering, on the right, a small closed chapel contains the fifteenth century

▲▼ *Sé, the Upper Choir and the two Baroque organs*

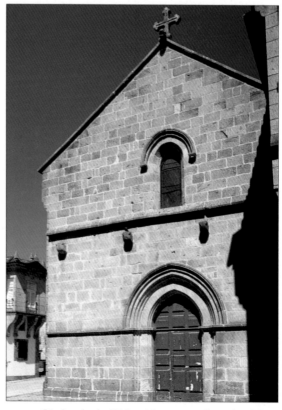

▲ *Sé, Capela da Glória with entrance from the cloister*

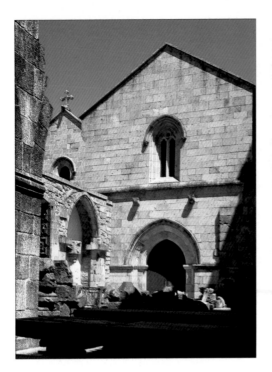

◄▲ *Sé, Capela de São Geraldo and the tombs of Henry of Burgundy and his wife Teresa, in the Capela dos Reis*

From the square eighteenth century **Cloister**, one enters the chapels and the Museu de Arte Sacra. The **Capela da Glória** is a triumph of Mudejar azulejos and bas reliefs, while the **Capela de São Geraldo**, or St. Gerard's Chapel, dedicated to the first archbishop of Braga (1096-1108), is entirely covered with frescoes.

The Gothic **Capela dos Reis** contains the tombs of Henry of Burgundy and his wife Teresa, and of the archbishop of Braga Dom Lourenço Vicente who fought in the battle of Aljubarrota, at the time of the *Reconquista*. The **Museu de Arte Sacra**, with its **Treasury**,

is on the upper floor, and contains precious sacerdotal vestments embroidered with threads of gold, sculpture, solid silver chalices and a monstrance in gilded silver with four hundred fifty diamonds. There is also a crèche by Machado de Castro and a small iron cross of great symbolic value. It was used in celebrating the first mass in Brazil after it was discovered. There are also countless jewels, which were donated. A curiosity is a pair of men's shoes with heels about twelve centimeters high. They are extremely elegant silk shoes and belonged to the Archbishop Dom Rodrigo da Cunha, who was only one meter twenty tall.

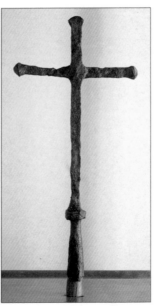

◄ *Sé, Museu de Arte Sacra, the iron cross used in celebrating the first mass in Brazil just after it had been discovered*

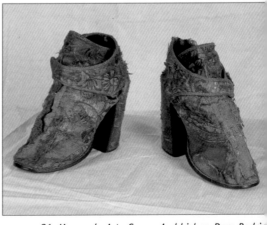

▲ *Sé, archaeological finds in the cloister*

▲ *Sé, Museu de Arte Sacra, Archbishop Dom Rodrigo da Cunha's high-heeled shoe*

The old **Paço dos Arcebispos**, the former Episcopal palace, is behind the Sé, in *Largo do Paço*. It is a complex consisting of three fourteenth and seventeenth century buildings. Inside is a precious **municipal library** and **archives** with documents and records going as far back as the ninth century. All of Braga's ancient history is jealously conserved in these rooms. At the back of the palace is the **Jardim de Santa Bárbara** with a *chafariz* (fount) which legend says was visited by the saint.

The **Câmara Municipal**, or town hall, behind the Paço dos Arcebispos, is an eighteenth century structure with a Baroque facade by the architect André Soares da Silva. At the center of the square is a large Baroque fountain, known as the **Pelican Fountain**.

To the north is the **Igreja do Pópulo**, never empty no matter what time of the day it may be. It was built by the Jesuit archbishop Frei Agostinho de Jesus after 1535 in honor of the Virgin Mary to whom he was particularly devoted. The church was once part of an Augustinian convent and was later ren-ovated, to which the Baroque facade by Carlos Amarante, an architect from Braga, bears witness. The sober interior has side chapels and a nave. The white and blue azulejos, including those in the **Sacristy**, are by Bernardes.

▼ *Jardim de Santa Bárbara behind the Paço dos Arcebispos*

▲ *The Cámara Municipal, by André Soares da Silva, and the Sala Nobre, inside*

▼ *Capela de Nossa Senhora da Conceiç*
and Capela dos Coimbr

◄ *The popular Igreja do Pópulo*

▲ *Palacete do Raio, a Rococo gem known as the Casa do Mexicano*

The seventeenth century **Igreja de Santa Cruz**, a curious example of mannerist Baroque, merits a visit, as does the **Capela de Nossa Senhora da Conceição**, of 1525, with statues of Saint Anthony and Saint Paul. The *Deposition*, a sculpture of the school of Coimbra, is magnificent.

Also to be seen is the sixteenth century **Capela dos Coimbras** with its Manueline tower, and decorations of statues and a faun. Next to it is the **Solar dos Coimbras**. **Palacete do Raio**, a Rococo gem, is known as the *Casa do Mexicano*, with a facade of blue azulejos. The **Palácio dos Biscainhos** is also a noble sixteenth century residence and now houses the **Museu Etnográfico dos Biscainhos**. The entrance with its flagstones and eighteenth century statues was the carriageway to the stables.

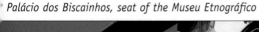

Palácio dos Biscainhos, seat of the Museu Etnográfico

▼ *The museum entrance with its stone paving and eighteenth century statues*

▲ *Museu dos Biscainhos, Sala de Jantar (Dining Room) and Sala Nobre (Reception Hall)*

Nowadays the visitor is received by a recording of the sound of horses. The rooms with the paintings, silver, porcelains, furniture collected there, give us an idea of the life of the sixteenth century Portuguese nobility. The **Dining Room** has elegant frescoes on the walls, while the **Reception Hall** has a splendid painted wooden ceiling, with azulejos with scenes of the hunt and life in the fields on the walls. A curiosity is the **Woman's Room**, with a small altar. This was a harem or secluded part of the house where the wife of the owner withdrew, while her husband was engaged in his business affairs. The terraced gardens, with a fountain and many statues, low hedges and countless flowers, are a marvel. They include rare species and exotic plants, such as a *tulip tree* from Virginia which has been flourishing for two hundred and eighty years.

The surroundings of Braga are also bound to the faith. In São Jerónimo Real, a hamlet only three kilometers from Braga, is the charming **Capela de São Frutuoso de Montélios**, perhaps the only example of Byzantine architecture in Portugal, with Visigothic and Mozarabic influences. The latter is an art that derives from the fusion of the Visigoths, who arrived in Lusitania in the sixth century, with the new Arab conquerors. It was built in the eighth century by the archbishop of Braga, Frutuoso de Dume, was partially destroyed by the Arabs and rebuilt in the twelfth century. The interior is very simple, completely without decoration, and contains the cenotaph of Saint Fructuosus, whose remains were taken to the neighboring Baroque church of São Francisco.

The **Mosteiro de São Martinho de Tibães**, six kilometers from Braga, is however quite another thing. This majestic monastery, the mother house of the Portuguese and Brazilian Benedictine monks, is clearly visible from a distance. The monastery, built in the eleventh century, was restored in the nine-

◄ *Capela de São Frutuoso in the hamlet of Montélios*

Mosteiro de São Martinho de Tibães, the Rua das Fontes and a view of the gardens

teenth and is currently once more under restoration. Declared a national monument, the State in collaboration with the European Union will install a historical museum on the premises. The Greek-cross church is truly lovely. It is a triumph of Baroque in the art of *talha dourada*. It has a nave only, with a vaulted ceiling and a dazzling golden high altar. There are numerous paintings on the walls of the **Sacristy**, portraits of eighth century Benedictine monks. The azulejos in the **Chapter Hall** are seventeenth century. The splendid historical gardens, open to the public, take us along an itinerary with many species of plants, such as the gigantic blue hortensias more than a hundred years old, to the pond and the **Escadório** or **Rua das Fontes**, a stepped path with many fountains leading to the highest fountain or Paradise, the way of salvation for believers.

▶ *Mosteiro de São Martinho de Tibães, the sumptuous Baroque interior of the church*

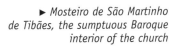

FROM THE ROMARIAS TO FÁTIMA
The ancient and profound faith of the Portuguese

Out of a population of ten million, 95% of the Portuguese are of the Catholic faith. They live together with a small community of two thousand Jews, about twenty thousand Muslims and Orthodox, Protestant, Anglican, Mormon, Jehovah's Witnesses and Evangelical minorities. Religion and the influence of the Catholic Church are stronger in the north.

The city of Braga has forty-five churches and many shrines. From its beginnings it was an important bishop's see and merits the title of the Portuguese "Rome-Vatican".

Religion thus is still important in this country, despite the fact that changes and transformations are in course. The Church remains the place of worship and meeting for the community and participation in Sunday services is usual above all in the north.

Participation in the Romarias, the festivals and celebrations of religious significance and almost always dedicated to the patron saint or the Virgin Mary are strongly felt. Again it is the North which can boast of the most solemn and spectacular Romarias, especially those

dedicated to the Passion of Christ in Holy Week, or that of Nossa Senhora da Agonia in Viana do Castelo on the day of the Assumption. These festivals are often accompanied by folk music in traditional costumes, with gastronomic feasts and rivers of wine.

Pilgrimages and devotion for the Virgin of Fátima is of prime importance. The Marian cult is strongly rooted and the figure of the Virgin in her various representations plays a central role in religious practice. Even so at times the Church has opposed itself with orthodox rigor to a popular religiosity which in certain celebrations takes on the forms of ancient pagan rites.

From Christianity on, the history and politics of Portugal were closely connected with religious faith: from the Reconquista in which the Crusaders played a part, to the arrival of the Cistercian monks who made a determining contribution to the creation of a new architecture and the diffusion of agriculture. Nor must one forget that the first descobertas were financed by the Templar Knights, later the Order of Christ: the Cross of the Order of Christ and the Armillary Sphere were the symbols of King Manuel I, a sign that the period of conquests was considered above all a religious crusade. With the wealth that flowed in from the new lands, palaces and sumptuous monuments were built, but also cathedrals, churches and shrines, monasteries and abbeys. One of the marks of this opulence was the decoration known as talha dourada, wood carved and covered with large amounts of gold, almost always in the prevailing Baroque style.

EX-VOTO A Nossa Senhora do Porto Seguro de Cascaes, no regreço da faina, roze Borges e filho Diogo Salvos por terem apego á Santa. N. S. P. S. 60 dias indulgencias. R.R.A.M.S.R. ANO 1745

Always in the name of religion, the Inquisition was introduced into Portugal upon request of the Jesuits in 1531 by João III, the pious king. And more recently, in the name of faith and above all in view of the prophesies of the Virgin at Fátima, the profoundly Catholic head of State Salazar chose neutrality and Portugal was kept out of the horrors of World War II.

▲ *Bom Jesus do Monte*

BOM JESUS DO MONTE

The three neighboring shrines of Bom Jesus do Monte, Sameiro and Santa Marta da Falperra form a triangle of faith, devotion, pilgrimage, including tourism, and are only six kilometers from Braga.

Sameiro is the shrine dedicated to the Virgin of the Immaculate Conception, the **Imaculada Conceição**, erected after Pope Pius IX had declared the "dogma of the Immaculate Conception" on December 8, 1854. A statue of Pius IX is in the small church square. After Fátima, it is the most important site of Marian devotion in Portugal, while that of Santa Marta da Falperra has a Baroque **chapel** dedicated to **Saint Magdalene**, where pilgrims go to pray after the processions.

But the most famous of the three is **Bom Jesus do Monte**. Universally recognized as a gem of Portuguese Baroque art, it is also the most imposing Baroque *Via Crucis* or Way of the Cross. More people come here than anywhere else and in the *Semana Santa* or Holy Week, the haunting moving celebration of the Passion of Christ, immense crowds flock to the shrine. Many leave ex-voto, notes, gifts and candles in the shape of human organs. The most devoted climb the *Escadaria* up to the church on their knees.

The Bom Jesus is in a splendid panoramic position, on a slope at an altitude of five hundred meters, on Mount Espinho. Surrounded by oak woods and silence, there are paths, a lake and flourishing gardens in an area of five hundred and two hectares. The shrine was built by the archbishop of Braga Dom Rodrigo de Moura Telles, who entrusted the work to Carlos Amarante, the architect from Braga who represents the passage from the Baroque to Neoclassicism in Portugal.

▼ *Bom Jesus do Monte, the Escadaria, monument to the Baroque*

▲▶ *Facade and interior of the church*

walls plastered white, where perspective plays a leading role. It is a double staircase with crossed balustrades and the six hundred fifty-four steps symbolize the difficult ascent of man towards God, the elevation of the spirit.

The chapels along the *Escadaria* represent the *Stations of the Cross* with life-size statues, and numerous fountains. The water is a metaphor of the spring of life, purification of the spirit and of the body. The *Spring of the Five Senses* consists of five fountains which personify sight, hearing, touch, taste and smell.

The *Strairway of the Three Theological Virtues* on the other hand is adorned with allegorical statues, symbols of Faith, Hope and Charity. If you focus on the fountains from below, from the Portico, the whole has the shape of a great chalice. The *Via Crucis* begins in the **Portico** with the two side chapels of the *Last Supper* and *Christ in the Garden of Gethsemane*. On the crenellated portico, flanked by two fountains with

The Neoclassic **church** stands on the site of a small chapel. The austere building has two bell towers at the sides and eight statues including *Herod* and *Pilate*.

Inside in the **Capela do Bom Jesus** is a wooden figure of the suffering *Christ*, and the walls are covered with notes, ex-voto, many "wax babies" (in memory of those who died early) and even a miniature caravel. On the high altar is a *Crucifixion* in bronze. In the **Sacristy** is a collection of portraits of the many benefactors of the shrine from all over the world.

The most famous attraction of the Bom Jesus do Monte is the immense **Escadaria**, the scenic Baroque stairway in stone, its

the symbols of the sun and moon, is the coat of arms of the archbishop founder. The words *"Jerusalém Santa restaurada e reedificada no ano de 1723"* are written on the fountain of the sun, while on the other is *"pelo ilustríssimo Senhor Dom Rodrigo de Moura e Telles Arcebispo Primaz"*.

While the devotion of some pilgrims is so intense that they climb the entire *Escadaria* on their knees, for those who cannot or do not wish to climb to the top on foot, there is a handy funicular in the square of the Portico. This yellow tram, the *Elevador*, has been taking visitors and pilgrims up to the church in only four minutes for a hundred and eighteen years. It is the only extant example in the world which still runs on water.

▲ *The Elevador which takes pilgrims and visitors to the church*

▼ *The Capela do Bom Jesus with the wooden Christ and the ex-votos*

▲ *The magnificent gardens of the Sanctuary*

GUIMARÃES

The words *"Aqui nasceu Portugal"* are written on the walls of medieval Guimarães. Here Portugal was born, and this is why it is called *Berço da Nação*, the cradle of Portugal. In 1110 Afonso Henriques, first king of Portugal, was born here, and it was from here when he was only twenty years old that he began the long *Reconquista* against the Arabs who were defeated and driven out in the memorable battle of Ourique of 1139 (Lisbon was conquered in 1147). Another famous Portuguese, Gil Vicente, humanist and dramatist and considered the father of the Portuguese theater, was born here in 1470.

Guimarães has fifty thousand inhabitants and is located at the foot of the Serra de Santa Catarina mountains. The entire city is like an enormous park, full of flowers, luxuriant trees and well tended streets. It is the seat of the University and of a soccer team. The economy is flourishing with a wealth of industries and crafts with textile factories and cutlery works, workshops where leather and wicker are worked as well as gold and silver. Marvelous examples of embroidery are still made by hand, above all on linen, an old tradition which dates to the Middle Ages. Fine linen, in demand on the international market, is produced here.

▲ *Largo da Oliveira, with its cafes and old houses*

▲ *Houses in the old city and illuminations*

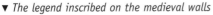

▼ *The legend inscribed on the medieval walls*

▲ *Paço do Concelho, with its Gothic arches*

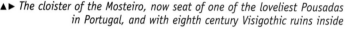
▲▶ *The cloister of the Mosteiro, now seat of one of the loveliest Pousadas in Portugal, and with eighth century Visigothic ruins inside*

Anyone wanting to spend a night to dream of and be at peace with the world, and where money is no problem, should stay at one of the splendid old palaces, or *Pousadas*, the epitome of beauty and elegance with all modern comforts. Guimarães has the most beautiful *Pousadas* in all of Portugal. One of the most elegant is the **Pousada de Santa Marinha da Costa**, on a hill with a marvelous view seven kilometers from the town center, in the monastery with the samer name. The church itself is open to the public and there is a Visigothic ruin dating to the eighth century in the cloister with a fountain at the center. The veranda is completely lined with eighteenth century azulejos, by master Policarpo de Oliveira Bernardes. The wife of Afonso Henriques had the **Mosteiro de Santa Marinha da Costa** built in 1154 by the Augustinian order in gratitude to the patron saint of pregnant women, Santa Marinha.

The Pousada has an excellent restaurant with a tasty *minhota* cuisine based on meat, a specialty is *Sarrabulho*, boiled beef, pork and fowl with rice, cottage cheese with fine herbs and spices.

Guimarães, which was the Celtic Wimara and then became Roman, developed above all in the twelfth century with Henry of Burgundy, father of Afonso Henriques, count of Portucale (region between the Minho and the Douro), who had many buildings constructed and set his residence there. The monuments of Guimarães bear witness to this happy medieval past and the town center is a tangle of lanes, alleys, stairs and tree-lined small squares.

◀ *Mosteiro de Santa Marinha da Costa*

The **Castelo** rises up above on the Sagrada hill, in defense of the city. The tenth century structure is square in form, and the oldest monument in the city, with eight imposing crenellated towers and a large **Torre de Menagem**, the keep, inside which are the remains of the fortress. It was enlarged two centuries later by Henry of Burgundy, and according to tradition this is where the future king was born. The small Romanesque church of **São Miguel do Castelo** in one wing of the castle still has the **baptismal font** where Afonso Henriques was baptized. Leaving the Castelo and crossing the public park and *Largo do Toural*, the square, vital center of the city with banks, restaurants, hotels, and the fine patrician homes, leads you to **Paço dos Duques**, of the dukes of Braganza and Guimarães. The palace, which was long the residence of the last dynasty of the Lusitanian sovereigns, was built in the fifteenth century. When the court moved to a larger holding in Vila Viçosa in the sixteenth century, the palace fell into ruin. The Braganza dynasty governed the country for two hundred seventy years and the last king, Manuel II, fled into exile in 1910.

▲ *The Castelo de São Miguel on the Sagrada hill*

The Paço dos Duques, after a series of rather unfortunate attempts at restoration, now houses a museum while part of it is the residence reserved for the president of the Portuguese Republic.

The palace can be identified by a series of slender chimneys in red brick. It consists of four blocks with towers which surround the cloister. Inside, the taste and elegance of the court are on display in the rows of rooms which house splendid Flemish and French

Igreja de São Miguel

▼ *Paço dos Duques de Bragança*

fifteenth and sixteenth century tapestries, Aubusson and Gobelin tapestries, antique and Indo-Portuguese furniture, and fine silver and Chinese porcelain. In the **Armory Hall** there is a valuable seventeenth century collection of weapons. There is a magnificent wooden ceiling and the overturned hull of a caravel in the **Banquet Hall,** with paintings and portraits by Dutch and Italian painters on the walls. The royal Braganza coat of arms is over the Gothic portal of the **Capela do Paço,** which contains holy images and paintings by Josefa de Óbidos, the Portuguese woman painter inside.

▼ *Igreja de Nossa Senhora da Oliveira with the Gothic bell tower and the Padrão do Salado, fourteenth century Gothic shrine*

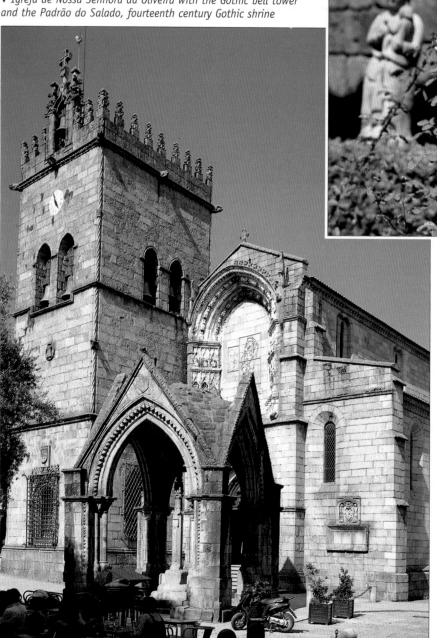

▲ *Sculptures in the cloister of Nossa Senhora da Oliveira, seat of the Museu de Alberto Sampaio*

▲ *Museu de Alberto Sampaio, the suit worn by King João I in the battle of Aljubarrota in 1385*

Continuing towards the city center in the medieval paved square of *Largo da Oliveira*, the soul of the old city with old houses with wrought iron terraces, one comes to the **Igreja de Nossa Senhora da Oliveira**. A portal with a Gothic pediment and a Gothic window bear witness to the original building, while the Manueline **bell tower** dates to 1505. The Baroque dominates in the church with its nave and two aisles. The fourteenth century silver altar is a fine piece of silverwork. There is a Gothic shrine, the **Padrão do Salado**, with a fourteenth century stone crucifix, on the square facing the church. According to tradition this is where an olive branch which had been brought from the Mount of Olives in Jerusalem by a pilgrim miraculously came to life. The Romanesque **cloister** of the church of Nossa Senhora da Oliveira which houses the **Museu de**

▲ *Convento de São Domingos, the Gothic cloister, now seat of the Museu de Martins Sarmento*

Alberto Sampaio is a masterpiece, in the words of the Portuguese writer José Saramago "…for its irregularity of design and the secluded air". The arches and columns have elaborate Moorish capitals and the museum contains one of the most important collections of religious images in Portugal, gold and silver chalices, monstrances, reliquaries, paintings, sculpture and frescoes which belonged to the church **Tesouro** or Treasury. There is also a silver triptych with *Nativity scenes*, donated by King João I together with the garment the king wore in the battle of Aljubarrota in 1385.

The **Museu de Martins Sarmento**, the other important museum in the city, is in *Rua de Paio Galvão* near *Largo do Toural* and is also in a fine Gothic cloister of the fourteenth century **Convento Igreja de São Domingos**. It contains prehistoric finds, coin collections and contemporary art. Worthy of note is a stone sculpture three meters high with an arm upraised known as the **Colossus de Pedralva**, and the door of the crematory furnace of the *Citânia de Briteiros* known as **Pedra Formosa**, that is beautiful stone, with interlaced garlands and geometric friezes.

◄ *Colossus de Pedralva, stone sculpture three meters high*

Two other churches in Guimarães also merit a visit: the **Igreja de São Francisco** and the **Igreja dos Santos Passos**. The latter, surrounded by splendid flowering gardens and flanked by two Baroque bell towers, has a façade decorated with sculpture and paintings with scenes from the *Passion of Christ* framed in mother of pearl in the interior. The Igreja de São Francisco dedicated to the saint of Assisi was built in the early 1400s but subsequently modified. The life of the saint is narrated in the capitals of the portal.

▲ *View of the Igreja de São Francisco with the portal of the oratory of the same name, faced in blue azulejo tiles, in the foreground*

The Baroque re*table* in *talha dourada* and eighteenth century azulejo decorations with the *Story of the Saint* is particularly fine. There are precious gilded wooden sculptures and a fine coffered wooden ceiling in the **Sacristy** while the Renaissance **Cloister** is one of the later additions.

The best way to appreciate the beauty of the city is to take the *teleférico da Penha*, a cablecar which takes one to the highest point of the Serra de Santa Catarina, right on the hill of Pena at an altitude of six hundred meters. The panorama seen from this *miradouro* is absolutely stupendous.

◄ *Igreja dos Santos Passos in the midst of splendid gardens*

Talha Dourada

▲ The elaborate ceiling of the Igreja de São Francisco in Porto

*T*he word Baroque is Portuguese, and literally means "an irregularly shaped pearl".

The art form of the Portuguese-Brazilian Baroque is the "talha dourada", or carved and gilded wood.

The most important material for talha dourada is gold, which flowed into Portugal in great quantities from the new colonial possession discovered "by chance" by the navigator **Pedro Álvares Cabral** in 1500, which was later named Brazil from a kind of dyewood, pau-brasil, found there.

The typical characteristics of this Portuguese and Brazilian art are the use of plant motifs, cherubs and winged angels, shells, feathers, garlands and allegorical figures. As is true of Western Europe in general, this art too occupies an important place in Catholic religious symbolism and the Eucharist, with leaves and bunches of grapes, acanthus leaves, flowers, birds, diabolic figures and scenes of daily life, all part of this splendid tangle of elements, narrative and artistic, which also turns into an intimate exchange between the work of art and the observer who loses himself in the artistic world glowing with gold.

▼ Side chapel in talha dourada in the Igreja de Santa Clara in Porto

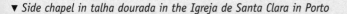

The Baroque itself as art took hold in Portugal-Brazil later (as much as a century later, in the eighteenth century when the rest of Western Europe was already turning to Neoclassicism). The underlying reason was that preceding art styles had hung on longer and because politically Portugal had to reacquire and reinforce its national independence from Spain. In Western Europe with this new artistic concept, the idea of a "dynamically created space, of flexible walls, with an alternating play of convexity-concavity, now contracted, now illusionistically dilated, in which space is annulled, the antithesis of interior and exterior" (free translation from Heinrich Wölfflin, Renaissance and Baroque, 1888).

For scholars the phrase which affirms: "Baroque is always the non style, the unshapeliness, of what has gone before", "but in the continuance of an artistic evolution, one cannot disregard this unshapeliness."

VILA REAL

Vila Real lies in a splendid position: on a hill, surrounded by the geometrically terraced vineyards, at the foot of the Serras do Marão e do Alvão (the Nature Park), where the two rivers Rio Corgo and Rio Cabril meet. Together with the neighboring localities of Pinhão and Peso da Régua they form the golden triangle of *Vinho do Porto*, white and red, and above all the famous rosé that the world knows by the name of *Mateus*.

The city is the capital of the Trás-os-Montes region, which literally means "behind the mountains", the most desolate, harsh and inaccessible zone in all of Portugal, where the people are dignified in their poverty, leave the doors of their homes open, and are cordial and ready to help. This is a fascinating region, waiting to be discovered by the more discerning tourist.

Vila Real with its twenty-five thousand inhabitants lives on commerce, agriculture and crafts. In the small hamlet of **Bisalhães**, five kilometers distant, the famous black stoneware is made, the *Pucarinhos*, to be painted in bright colors and sold during the **Festa de São Pedro** which the city celebrates on June 28 and 29.

Vila Real, unlike Oporto, a city of middle class entrepreneurs, has always been favored by the Lusi-tanian aristocracy, and the name, given to it in 1283 by its founder, King Dom Dinis I, a patron king who promoted letters, arts and agriculture, does after all mean "royal city". The navigator Diogo Cão, who discovered the Congo, was born in Vila Real and the Portuguese writer Camilo Castelo Branco (1825-1890) who wrote *Amor de Perdição* (Love of Perdition), also chose to live here. He was a typical romantic genius with an obsessive and impetuous temperament who in the end took his own life. The city has a well preserved historical center, with its old streets, many noble palaces, their facades decorated with coats of arms. It also contains the remains of the **Pánois**, a Roman temple of the first century A.D., dedicated to Serapis, god of the Underworld. Excavations around this temple in the **Vale das Nogueiras**, have brought to light stone altars for human sacrifices and numerous tablets with inscriptions in Latin.

Avenida de Carvalho Araújo is the main street of the city flanked not only by the **Casa de Diogo Cão** at number 19, but also by the **Paço Municipal**, a nineteenth century building with a monumental staircase, and the **Sé Catedral de São Domingos**. This Gothic convent church of the Dominican friars is in stone and has a nave and two aisles. It still has its Romanesque capitals. The **Igreja dos Clérigos** or **Capela de São Pedro** has a sumptuous Baroque facade by the Italian architect Nicola Nasoni, and the blue and white azulejos on the inside are also outstanding. But the real attraction for tourists in the surroundings of Vila Real is the **Solar de Mateus**, the splendid Baroque noble residence which has become a symbol and is even to be found on the label of one of the famous rosé wines, the Mateus. It is an elegant building with a double staircase, spires and pinnacles, articulated with gray stone and white plaster. The proportions of this building by Nicola Nasoni are perfect. The sumptuous rooms contain important paintings of Italian school; the ceilings are completely covered with frescoes; the furniture is in fine wood, and a collection of Ming vases stands in the imposing dining room.

The great basin, almost a pool, in which the entire palace is mirrored, dates to 1930, as do the splendid Italianate gardens. Here in the garden of marvels there are camellias, hortensias, roses, hibiscus, orchards, box hedges and cedars, forming a *bower* thirty-five meters long beyond which the terraced vineyards begin.

◄ *Solar de Mateus, the splendid Italian-style gardens*

▲ *Solar de Mateus, Baroque work by Nicola Nasoni*

AMARANTE

Amarante is a charming provincial town, one of the most joyous in Northern Portugal. It is a city of wine where the *vinho verde* is produced. It is also the city of São Gonçalo, the saint born at the end of the twelfth century, protector of love, lovers and couples, and as the writer José Saramago says, "Amarante seduces its guests with feminine arts".

The first weekend of June the city celebrates its highly popular patron saint who it is said loved to organize parties and dances so the women would find husbands and not be prey to temptation.

For the festival Amarante blossoms out in lights and colored garlands with games, tournaments, agricultural fairs, crafts, songs, dances and fireworks. The procession and the celebration of the *Romaria* mark the end of the spree. Lovers renew their promises, while singles pray to the saint to meet their soul

◄▲ *View of the Igreja and Mosteiro de São Gonçalo*

mates. Sweets and propitiatory cookies are exchanged. They are called *Bolos de Gonçalo*, and are made with butter, eggs, cinnamon and flour.

Amarante is seventy kilometers from Oporto, at the foot of the Serra do Marão, on the banks of the Tâmega River, surrounded by hills with terraced vineyards. A traditionally romantic city, it has a historical center with many lovely sixteenth and seventeenth houses with loggias and balconies in painted wood and wrought iron overlooking the lanes and riverside, with a scattering of elegant shops and cafés. There is an old stone bridge with three spans, a tranquil navigable river with swans and five minutes from the center, the **Praça de Touros** for the *tourada* on holidays.

Archaeological finds bear witness to the fact that Amarante was already a settlement in the fourth century B.C. Although the inhabitants, who firmly keep faith with São Gonçalo, an ascetic who lived in the area, ascribe the birth of the city to him, the construction of the first bridge on the Tâmega River (which was swept away in a flood in 1763) and a church built on the site of his hermitage.

In the lively market square, **Praça da República**, is the **Igreja** and **Mosteiro de São Gonçalo** built between 1540 and 1620 for King João III. The church, with a red brick dome decorated with azulejos, is rather severe. There is a statue of São Gonçalo in a niche n the stone façade, while in a loggia near the side doorway are the statues of the Portuguese kings who helped found the church. The Baroque interior was modified around the eighteenth cen-

▲ *Igreja de São Gonçalo, the Tomb of the Saint*

Igreja de São Gonçalo, wooden statues

tury and is typically in *talha dourada*, with two finely worked *pulpits* facing each other. The late seventeenth century organ supported by gilded allegorical figures is also superb. In the **Capela das Oferendas** (Chapel of the Offerings), to the left of the choir, is the tomb of São Gonçalo who died in 1259, with many gifts and ex-votos in wax, offerings made by the pious to their patron saint.

The interesting **Museu Amadeu de Sousa Cardoso** in the old convent cloister (entrance is on *Praça da República*) contains important finds of Roman date. Also noteworthy are the paintings and portraits by the cubist painter Amadeu de Sousa Cardoso, who was born in Amarante (1887-1918).

Sailing along the Douro

▲ View of Vila Nova de Gaia with the Mosteiro da Serra do Pilar and the ferry for excursions on the Douro River

*N*o river has ever been as synonymous as this with the city through which it runs: it makes no difference whether you say Oporto or Douro. A strong deep bond joins the historical vicissitudes and life of the city to its river from the very beginning. Oporto owes its fortune and prosperity to the Douro River, the river of gold (for the water glitters gold in the sun). The city rises on the right bank, five kilometers from the sandy mouth on that happy stretch in which the Douro curves twice forming gentle loops before emptying its waters into the Atlantic.

The Douro, nine hundred eighty kilometers long, springs as the Duero in the Sierra de Urbión in Spain, and for a hundred kilometers marks the boundary between the two countries. It runs in Portugal for two hundred kilometers through a granite and schist valley, deep and narrow in the Alto Douro, terraced with vineyards, of the famous vinho do Porto, in an overall area of two hundred square kilometers, from Barqueiros (Mesão Frio) to Barca de Alva. It was the Marquês de Pombal who first designated this area in 1756 as the Região Demarcada do Douro.

The river was once a succession of rapids and one had to move up the river countercurrent. Then in collaboration with Spain five dams were built, to make it safe and navigable up to Barca de Alva, on the Spanish border.

The Douro valley is one of the favorite haunts of international tourism. A fascinating way to go upriver is to sail for a day on the steamships which leave from **Praça da Ribeira** in Oporto for **Barqueiros** or **Pinhão**. For Romantic souls and lovers there are weekly cruises on hotel-barges which leave from Oporto and arrive at the Spanish border. Once the Douro was the river route for the Rabelos, barges with flat bottoms so they could go over the rapids, which transported barrels of wine from Alto Douro to the wine lodges of Vila Nova

PANORAMA DO PINHÃO

◄ View of Pinhão in the early twentieth century, azulejo in the railroad station of Pinhão

de Gaia. Today tourists in their cruises can visit **Pinhão** and the town of **Peso da Régua** which lives for and from wine, and which was already the point of departure in the eighteenth century for the Rabelos. Pinhão is famous for the beautiful azulejos which face the station of the city and depict scenes of bucolic life.

The best times to visit the entire valley are spring, when the vines are green and flourishing, and autumn for the vintage and the countryside which is clothed in stupendous colors at that time of year.

The landscape that

▲ The Douro Valley with its terraced vineyards

passes by as the boats move along the river is splendid, with its hills and their geometric terraced vineyards, dotted here and there by white Quintas, the farms and residences of the wine producers, open to the public and where the best wines can be tasted. Of old the Quintas were out of bounds for women.

They were furnished very simply and austerely, with the bare minimum: a wrought iron bed, the fireplace in the kitchen, tables for keeping track of accounts, no bathroom. The whole idea was to keep the ladies from accompanying their husbands and distract them from their ritual of wine.

▲ Landscape along the Douro River with the Quintas

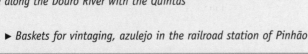

▶ Baskets for vintaging, azulejo in the railroad station of Pinhão

AVEIRO

▲ *The sandy beach of Costa No[...]*

Aveiro is a city of fifty thousand inhabitants on the Beira Litoral, that tongue of coast on the Atlantic, half way between Coimbra and Oporto.

With its many canals and hump-backed bridges, it is known, rather romantically, as the Lusitanian Venice or the Portuguese Amsterdam. It is located on the eastern bank of the Ria lagoon, at the mouth of the Rio Vouga, an enormous basin of sky-blue water which stretches out over six thousand hectares and from which countless canals branch off, with groups of gulls swooping over the water.

At dawn the landscape in this solitary silent lagoon, tinged with violet and full of eels, lost in the fog and halfway between land and water, is somehow metaphysical.

In summer there is nothing more pleasant than to go by boat along the fifty kilometers of the lagoon from Aveiro up to Torreira. The tour called *Rota da Luz* (route of light) crosses the entire lagoon, and the beaches up to the Ocean and takes you past salt pans, small fishing villages and pine groves.

▼ *Brightly colored houses on the Aveiro lagoon*

▲ *The Canal Central with eighteenth century palaces and Art Nouveau houses*

What fascinates tourists most about Aveiro is the vitality of the place, somehow softly unobtrusive, its luminosity and colors, found in the lovely eighteenth century palaces and Art Nouveau houses, in the squares, the old historical center, the low fishermen's houses in pastel hues which line the canals, the checkerboard salt pans with white mounds of salt and the brightly colored *Moliceiros*. These unique fishing boats decorated with primitive designs and ex-votos, have a flat bottom and a long curved prow similar to a sickle or the neck of an ostrich.

The traditional regatta of the *Moliceiros* on the occasion of the annual **Festa da Ria** which takes place in July and August attracts countless spectators and tourists to Aveiro for dances, songs and fiestas in the square.

Every boat is spanking clean and newly painted, for the prize is awarded not only to the winner of the regatta, but also to the most beautiful and extravagant *Moliceiro*.

The economy of the city, the third largest industrial center in Portugal after Lisbon and Oporto, depends in great part on the *Moliceiros*, used in the

▶ *Carcavedos Bridge on the Canal de São Roque*

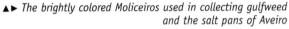
▲► *The brightly colored Moliceiros used in collecting gulfweed and the salt pans of Aveiro*

muddy lagoon for collecting the *moliço*, or gulfweed, which is an excellent natural fertilizer, the extraction and exportation of salt, the processing of cork.

Aveiro is also famous for its cuisine, with a long tradition of dishes using meat and fish such as the *Enguias fritas* and the *Caldeirada de enguias* (fried eel and eel stew), not to speak of the cod, processed in firms like that of *Manuel Marques (Rua do Vale Caseiro Variante de Cacia)* as far back as the sixteenth century. In this farm-workshop, open to the public, one can watch the entire process leading up to the drying, and buy the best *bacalhau salgado verde*: the finest of dried cod.

Gourmands will delight in the *Ovos-Moles*, the soft sweets typical of Aveiro with a millenary tradition in the convents. These cream pastries, made with egg

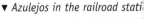
◄ *Facade of an Art Nouveau house*

▼ *Azulejos in the railroad stati*

Floor with decorative motifs

tants. Fortunes changed in 1808 however when another violent tide reopened the way to the sea and the city came back to life. It is divided by two main canals: the Canal Central and the Canal de São Roque. On the banks of the **Canal de São Roque** is the popular and picturesque **Beira Mar district**, with its alleys, lanes, fishermen's houses, and the **Mercado do Peixe** where the night's catch is auctioned off every morning. The historical buildings, eighteenth century palaces and Art Nouveau houses and those decorated with azulejos as well as the splendid **Praça Humberto Delgado** are in the area of the **Canal Central**. This is why Aveiro is called the city of the azulejos. The square is the vital city center, the point of arrival of one of the most beautiful and elegant tree-lined avenues, *Avenida Dr. Lourenço Peixinho*, the place to go shopping, with its pastry shops, bookstores, antique dealers and fashion boutiques.

South of the Canal Central is the paved **Praça da República** with the **Câmara Municipal**, an eighteenth century building, flanked by the sixteenth century **Igreja** and **Museu da Misericórdia**, the facade completely covered with azulejos and with a fine Renaissance portal. Of particular note in the small museum of sacred art is a standard which

yolk, sugar and butter and encased in a shell or fish-shaped wafer, are even celebrated in Portuguese literature. The *Pastelaria Avenida* (Dr. Lourenço Peixinho, 84) makes *Ovos-Moles* according to the original recipe and proposes inexpensive souvenirs to take home in the form of small decorated aluminum or wooden boxes containing twelve pastries.

Aveiro has been an Episcopal see from ancient times, and now is the seat of an important university and many cultural centers which promote events and fairs.

The city traded with the Phoenicians and was the Roman Talabriga. Traces of its past still exist in the stones and monuments, but practically nothing remains of the power that was and which came from the mining of salt, the *bacalhau* trade, the merchant city with its many comings and goings and with a great port on the Atlantic Ocean with caravels dropping and weighing anchor, their holds full to bursting.

It was a rich and flourishing city up to 1575 when a violent tidal wave silted up the harbor and Alveiro no longer found itself on the sea. This was the beginning of its decline and the exodus of its inhabi-

▶ *The facade of the Igreja da Misericórdia*

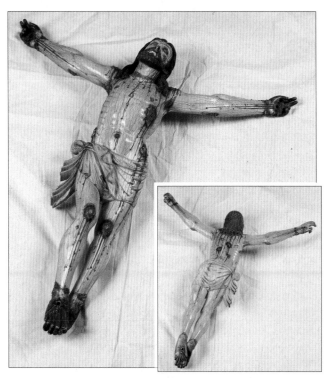

decorate the Baroque facade with its columns. Inside is a fine wooden *Madonna* and the sarcophagus of Caterina de Atayde, the *Natércia* woman sung and loved by the poet Luís de Camões. In front of the church is a tall column with a Manueline *Cruzeiro*, a cross set on a baldachin inlaid with scenes from the *Life of Christ*.

The Convento de Jesus of the Dominican nuns is the most representative monument in the city and houses the **Museu de Aveiro** with its important collections of art, precious objects, paintings, liturgical vestments, numerous decorated altars and statues. Of particular note is a unique statue of a suffering *Christ*, with oriental features and a body covered with wounds. They say it was carved in the city of Burgos by a Mudejar, an Arab converted to Christianity. The portrait of *Saint Joana*, painted by the great Portuguese painter Nuno Gonçalves, is splendid.

The **Convento de Jesus** was founded around 1461 and was where Princess Joana, whose father prohibited her from taking her vows, withdrew. She was beatified in 1693.

The interior of the church is truly sumptuous, a triumph of *talha dourada*, a technique of inlaid and

accompanied funeral processions, and the *Senhor da Índia*, a sixteenth century wooden Christ studded with rubies which symbolize his blood.

Continuing south on the Canal Central is the **Sé Catedral de São Domingos**, an austere church built in 1464 which was thoroughly renovated in the eighteenth century. Three statues of *Faith, Hope, Charity*

▶ Manueline cross on the column opposite the Cathedral

▼ Sé Catedral de São Domingos, sarcophagus of Catarina de Atayde, the woman Luís de Camões loved

Convento de Jesus, seat of the Museu de Aveiro

▶ Museu de Aveiro, Portrait of Saint Joana by Nuno Gonçalves

gilded wood, a typically Baroque Portuguese ornamental art. The **Chapel** with its facing of azulejos has a great deal of atmosphere and the choirs, the upper and the lower, are superb. The **Upper Choir** with its *talha dourada* decoration, has frescoed vaults and azulejos with episodes from the *Life of Saint Joana*, while the imposing tomb of the saint in polychrome marble and supported by statues of angels is in the **Lower Choir**. The monument is by the Portuguese João Antunes and took him twelve years to finish. Take particular note in the lower choir of the *lecterns* and the *chair* of the abbess, almost a throne in the elegance of the ornamentation.

The Renaissance **Cloister** in two levels, with benches where the sisters sat to pray, faced in azulejos, leads to the **Refectory** with its low wooden ceilings and walls faced with floral azulejos, and the **Chapter Hall**. Next to it is the Gothic tomb of Dom João de Albuquerque.

The **Sala de Lavor**, now a chapel with precious and elegant decorations in *talha dourada*, was the private room of the princess, patron saint of the city, where Joana spent her time praying and working, and where she died.

On leaving Aveiro an excursion of only a few kilometers north of the lagoon takes us to the lovely beaches of the Costa da Prata (silver coast) and Ovar.

Ovar is a city known for its carnival, its folklore floats, costumes and decorations which brighten the city during the **Festa de Carnaval**. A curious tradition has it that the name of the city comes from *varinhas* (fishmonger), applied to the wives of the fishermen and which was then contracted into *var*. It seems quite likely that the legend is more than just a legend for Ovar is a town whose life depends on fish and fishing.

◀ Museu de Aveiro, the tomb of the Princess Saint Joana

▲ *Convento de Jesus, the Upper Choir*

however, continues and is still a flourishing activity. In Ovar the picturesque houses and historical buildings are almost all decorated with brightly colored azulejo tiles, predominantly blue.

The city houses a small **Museu da Saudade** with pictures of bucolic scenes of life that was and the customs of the place. There is also a collection of African art of the former colonies. Tin addition the museum has a series of mementos of Júlio Dinis, a nineteenth century novelist who spent much of his life here.

The **Capela dos Passos** is the most important religious monument in Ovar. There are six chapels of the Calvary inside the church; the Stations of the Cross all decorated with wood

Early in the morning some fishing boats are still drawn up on the beach by oxen and then it is the women, bending over the nets, who sort out the fish and sell the catch at the market. Romantic and traditional scenes of this sort are becoming ever rarer, replaced by modernity and steel industries, naval yards and foundries. The extraction of salt,

and shell inlays. During Holy Week the moving procession of the *Passion of Christ*, with a millenary tradition, leaves from this church. This is also when the typical sweet dish of Ovar, the *Pão-de-ló*, is prepared and eaten. It is made mostly of eggs, using about twenty yolks and only five egg-whites, in addition to sugar and flour.

▲ *Convento de Jesus, the refectory*

▶ *A windmill in the countryside of Ovar*

CONÍMBRIGA

Roman Conímbriga is sixteen kilometers from Coimbra, in the village of Condeixa-a-Velha, along the most important Roman road which joined Olisipo to Sellium and to Bracara Augusta (Lisbon, Tomar, Braga). The archaeological site, surrounded by hills of olive trees, is one of the most important in Lusitania, and excavation seems to have no end.

The Romans settled here, probably on a Celtic settlement (Briga, of Celtic origin, means "defended territory") as early as the first century B.C. The emperor Augustus, and the subsequent dynasties, created an isle of superb civilization which enjoyed a long period of development and prosperity. Traces of a truly beautiful city still remain in Conímbriga and its spell-binding geometric monumentality bears witness to the greatness of Rome.

▲ *The Public Baths*

The city was also called Flavia Conímbriga (under the Flavian dynasty). It had monuments, baths, forums, an aqueduct and villas considered some of the finest in the Roman Empire of the West were built here. When the barbarian peoples arrived and the great Empire declined, the inhabitants erected high walls for defense along a perimeter of about two kilo-

Panorama of the archaeological area

meters. In 468, after numerous invasions and sacks, the Germanic Suebi arrived and destroyed almost all of it.

The **Museu Monográfico** has many rooms and numerous objects and finds which tell us of the refined taste, elegance and history of daily life in the ancient city. The

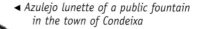

◄ Azulejo lunette of a public fountain in the town of Condeixa

of the fountains) with splendid gardens, many mosaics of hunting scenes and numerous fountains with jets of water which form geometric figures, and the **Casa Cantaber**, the largest, with its private baths, the ornamental basins

mosaics, fifteen hundred square meters of masterpieces, are of particular interest, as are the architectural remains, the sculpture and the frescoes, ceramics, coins and the model of the Flavian city.

Near the walls, facing each other, are the two loveliest patrician houses: the **Casa dos Repuxos** (House

with an ingenious system of subterranean heating. In one corner of the usual peristyle is a beautiful sculpture of *Perseus with the head of Medusa*.

The aqueduct, over three kilometers long, was built under Augustus, and brought in water from the spring of Alcabideque.

◄ *The House of the Fountains (Casa dos Repuxos)*

▼ *Casa Cantaber with its private bath*

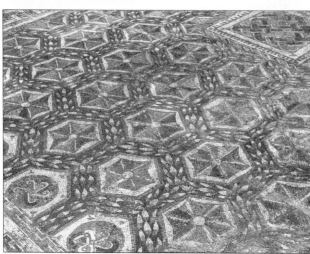

◄ *Detail of the splendid mosaic*

COIMBRA

Coimbra the learned, Coimbra temple of culture, of art, of science, Coimbra the regal, Coimbra first capital of Portugal, Coimbra bishop's see and center for the Inquisition. Along the road, at the entrance to the city, the visitor is welcomed by enormous posters with the words *"Coimbra Museu Civitade"* (Coimbra museum-city).

Coimbra is all this but also something else. The scepter of intellectual and cultural sovereignty has been in the hands of this city since the thirteenth century. With its millenary history and traditions, it is now also the third city of Portugal in importance and industrial development.

Coimbra is set against the hill of Alcaçova to keep watch over the Mondego River, the *Rio dos Poetas* as it is called here, on the road between Lisbon and Oporto.

▼ *View of the upper city*

▲ Escada de São Tiago   ▲ Moorish arch in the upper part of the city   ▲ Fado singers

This Lusitanian Athens with its ancient civilizations is full of monuments, churches, palaces which bear witness to its past and the winding cobbled streets, the lanes and alleys, the *becos*, and the stairs of the historical center wind along in a labyrinth as they climb up and down reminiscent of an Arab Medina: the urban layout inherited from the Moors.

The city is divided into Upper and Lower. Coimbra *Alta*, medieval, is the university and clerical part, of old the residence of the aristocracy; the *Baixa*, the lower city, is a crowded and popular area with shops, crafts, trade, cafés, restaurants, well tended avenues and parks.

Coimbra is a monochrome city, white (like Braga) with its gentle rhythms, marked by the university which governs from the Acropolis.

It is a seducing city where even the language, the Portuguese tongue, is pure and particularly melodious. Coimbra is a city full of contrasts, suspended between the past and the future, the old and the new, halfway between a university town and an industrial city, easy-going, frenetic, traditionalist, reformist. It is not large, but neither is it small. It is international but is still on a human scale, offers culture but also distractions. It is a city that tends to be rigorous, but with a sentimental soul perceptible in the fado *Quando Cai a Noite* (When night falls), with rhythm that is faster than the one sung in Lisbon, intellectual, ironic but full of poetry, different from Lisbon. In Coimbra the *fado* is only male, accompanied by a twelve stringed guitar. It is sung by students, by professors, by everyone, at every street corner, in the cafés or in the smoky *adegas* of this or that *becos*.

The city has always been an agricultural center and produces oil, wine and citrus fruits. Since the university alone was not enough to live on, it opened its doors to industry: textiles, food, leather tanning, factories for ceramics and pottery. But the feeling one has in this city is that the true soul of Coimbra is always the university, which with its rhythms, festivals, rites, marks the time and is what makes the people of Coimbra so alive, for when the twenty thousand students leave in summer they seem to fall into a sort of torpor. The end of the academic year in May is synonymous with a famous festival, as unconventional as students' festivals sometimes are, in which everyone takes part: the *Queima das Fitas*, the burning of the colored ribbons. Indeed every faculty has an identifying color of its own. The spectacular rite of the burning of the *fitas* on the steps of the old cathedral is performed by the graduating students wearing the severe black school uniform: *capa* and *batina*, tails and a long semicircular cape which makes them look like "bats" according to the writer Almeida Garrett, or "black angels" as Luís de Camões who studied here called them.

The origins of the city are Roman. They founded a *castrum* here and named it Aeminium. The splendid cryptoporticus of this period is now in the Museu de Machado de Castro. Coimbra however became important after the fall of the neighboring city of Conímbriga to the Germanic invaders and took the name Coimbra (contraction of Conímbriga) in the sixth century. Then the Moors came from the eighth to the twelfth century and it was called Almedina. With the *Reconquista* Coimbra was once more under Christian rule and in 1139, under Afonso Henriques, became the capital of Portugal. Its doors were opened to Arabs, Jews, men of letters, scientists, artists who came from everywhere to this humanist city, open to any and all debates and skilful mediator between Christians and the Muslims who were still in the South. A flourishing period during which it developed greatly followed for Coimbra and in 1308 the university was moved here from Lisbon. It was subsequently moved back to Lisbon, and returned definitively to Coimbra in 1537 and from then on the tie between the two has been indissoluble.

Illustrious scholars from all over Europe came to Coimbra to teach and its university competed with the most prestigious universities of Paris, Oxford, Bologna and Salamanca. A school of sculpture was also founded, with artists such as Nicolas Chanterène, Jean de Rouen, Machado de Castro (native of Coimbra), João and Diogo de Castilho whose contribution to the Portuguese Renaissance was determining. Coimbra became the center from which this art spread throughout the country.

To learn the secrets of the city and the spell it casts, you have to take long slow walks, beginning from the *Baixa*, in *Rua da Sofia*, named "street of wisdom" be-

▲ *Café Santa Cruz in Praça 8 de Maio*

cause of the many theological colleges located here. Two churches standing side by side look out on the street, the **Igreja do Carmo**, a convent parish church of 1597, and the **Igreja da Graça**, founded in 1543 by King João III.

Igreja do Carmo in Rua da Sofia known as the street of wisdom

▼ *Igreja da Graça in Rua da Sofia*

Continuing your walk you come to **Praça 8 de Maio**, crowded and alive with cafés, the haunt of actors and street artists, jugglers and students, above all in the splendid **Café Santa Cruz**, with its profusion of marbles and woodwork, located in the former convent chapel, and a tempting array of sweets, *pasteis de Santa Clara*, delicious crumbly cookies of sugar, eggs, butter, cinnamon and almonds, and the *touchinho do céu*, an exquisite convent cake of butter, eggs and almond paste.

The **Igreja Mosteiro de Santa Cruz** (next to the café) dominates the square. It is one of the most beautiful Catholic churches in the city. Founded between 1131 and 1132 by the friars of the Cross, followers of the rule of Saint Augustine, it was Dom Afonso Henriques who established its perimeter in writing, for it was not to be larger than the Sé Catedral. It was later renovated and enlarged by King Manuel I who entrusted the works to Diogo de Boytac and Nicolas Chanterène. A curiosity: Saint Anthony, who was born in Lisbon and died in Padua, received his intellectual and spiritual formation as well as his priestly orders in this church. Indeed, for two centuries this Convent was the cultural center where theology and medicine were taught. The Romanesque facade of Santa Cruz has a portal with rich decorations and Manueline and Mannerist sculpture. The luminous interior is a mixture of styles. The single nave is flanked by side chapels, and dominated by the great ribbed vault. There are enormous azulejo tile decorations on the walls which narrate the life of Saint Augustine and the completely carved Manueline *pulpit* is a superb work of art by Jean de Rouen decorated with statues of Saint Ambrose, Saint Augustine and the other Fathers of the Church. The organ dates to 1719 and was built in Portugal by the Spanish organ maker

◀▼ Igreja Mosteiro de Santa Cruz and the Manueline pulpit inside, richly sculptured by Jean de Rouen

◄▲ *Igreja de Santa Cruz, the tomb of King Afonso Henriques and the upper choir*

Manuel Benito Gómez Herrera. Facing each other, on either side of the high altar, are the tombs of King Afonso Henriques and his son Sancho I, with sumptuous decorations and fine chisel work. The monuments are respectively by Diogo de Castilho and by Nicolas Chanterène. On returning from a pilgrimage to Santiago de Compostela, King Manuel I ordered the mausoleum inside the church to be built.

The **Upper Choir** is one of the most interesting of its time with particularly beautiful benches in fine wood decorated with marine symbols representing the maritime adventures of the Portuguese pioneers. In the Renaissance **Sacristy** with its barrel vault there are the usual azulejos and important painting such as the *Pentecost*, a sixteenth century picture attributed to a Portuguese naïf artist, and the *Ecce Homo* and the *Crucifixion* by the painter Cristóvão de Figueiredo. The **Chapter Hall** leads to the **Claustro do Silêncio** (Cloister of Silence), in pure Manueline style with two orders of Gothic arches decorated with scenes of Calvary. The cloister was built by the architect Marcos Pires and has an elegant fountain at the center used by the monks as a lavabo before entering the refectory. The church has a **Sanctuary of Relics**, including some of Saint Augustine. The small **Jardim da Manga**, behind the Convent, is in a second cloister.

► *Igreja Mosteiro de Santa Cruz, the Cloister of Silence*

▲ Igreja de São Tiago

▲ Arco de Almedina, old Arab gate

Leaving Santa Cruz and continuing along *Rua Visconde da Luz*, one encounters **Praça do Comércio** surrounded by seventeenth and eighteenth century buildings and palaces. The large market used to take place here, and now on summer nights there are concerts of classic and folk music. The most important building is the Romanesque **Igreja de São Tiago**, currently closed for restoration. The square leads into *Rua Ferreira Borges* which ends in *Largo da Portagem*. This pedestrian street is the most important shopping center with the most fashionable shops, ranging from jewellery and goldwork to hardware and second-hand shops, as well as the ubiquitous *bacalhau* vendors.

There are two entrances for a visit to the old city above. One is the steps of the **Arco de Almedina**, the old gateway of the Arab fortress, the zone of

◄ *Rua Ferreira Borges,*
the characteristic street for shopping

the fado. The other has a bizarre name, the **Couraça de Lisboa** (cuirass of Lisbon), from *Largo da Portagem*. Both of them lead into a tangle of steep alleys of dark *becos* with laundry hung out to dry and where the sun is seen only now and then. Women sit out in the street, dogs and cats reign sovereign, the smell of wine, mold, misery and *sardinhas assadas* accompanies the visitor everywhere. These are places rich in humanity and secrets and distant suffering where another Coimbra comes to the fore, perhaps the real Coimbra, without the charismatic cloak of the university. One is spellbound and there is something in the air that reminds you of the Alfama and the Bairro Alto of Lisbon or the Ribeira of Oporto.

Crossing through this Medina one encounters the **Sé Velha**, the old cathedral of the city which looks more like a fortress than a Christian church. King Afonso Henriques had it built in the twelfth century and wanted it imposing to celebrate the victory over the Moors. Coimbra had become capital and at the time was on the boundary between the Christians of the north and the Muslims of the south. Art historians consider the Sé one of the finest Romanesque buildings in all of Portugal, despite the later restorations, as in the side portal, **Porta Especiosa** with a wealth of Renaissance decorations by Jean de Rouen, now deteriorating. The inside with a nave and two aisles is characterized by its opulence, with a retable of 1502 in fine *talha dourada* on the high al-

▲ *Sé Velha, apse side and the tower with its polychrome cupola*

tar, depicting the *Life of Jesus Christ*. The altarpiece in the **Capela do Santíssimo Sacramento** consists of a wealth of sculptural decoration with the figures of Christ and his Disciples, a work of 1566 by Jean de Rouen and his pupil Tomé Velho. Opposite the transept is a splendid Manueline **Baptismal Font**, also richly carved by Diogo Pires. A **Gallery** with two-light openings on arches crosses the two side aisles, while the **Cloister**, simpler in feeling, has Gothic arches and capitals decorated with figures of animals. The church contains numerous tombs, including that of a converted Arab, Sisinando, one of the first governors of Coimbra.

◀ *Sé Velha, the old cathedral of the city with the University above*

▲▼ *Sé Velha, Capela do Santíssimo Sacramento and baptismal font by Diogo Pires*

▼ *Casa de Sobre-Ripas with Maneuline windows and doors*

◄ *Sé Velha, the Romanesque-Gothic cloister*

In *Rua Sub-Ripas*, behind the Sé Velha, is the **Casa de Sobre-Ripas**, a fine sixteenth century private house with Manueline doors and windows, and a curious **Museu da Memória da Escrita** inside the medieval **Torre de Anto**. The museum contains a collection of original works, poetry, texts and documents of local men of letters and artists to whom Coimbra thus renders homage.

Continuing on our walk, still climbing up, along *Rua do Cabido* and then along *Couraça dos Apóstolos* to the Sé Nova, behind the university and attached to the Museu de Castro, we are struck by the writing on the walls, the banners and placards at the windows, the notes on the doors: these are the ***Repúblicas***, each of which has a name and a symbol. The

▼ *Sé Nova*

► *Museu Machado de Castro,*
Roman cryptoporticus

▼ *Sé Velha, talha dourada altarpiece*

▼ *Museu Machado de Cast*
painting of the Virgin Mary, Portuguese sch

Repúblicas were created in the regime of Salazar, who taught economy in Coimbra, and are lodgings for ten or twenty students with regulations of a community into which the police could not and does not enter. The student rebellions of 1962 and 1969 began in these walls.

The **Sé Nova**, a Baroque church built by the Jesuits in 1598 for their theological college, became the new cathedral of Coimbra when the Marquês de Pombal had them expelled from Portugal in 1759. The Latin-cross cathedral was built by the architect Baltasar Alves on the model of the Gesù in Rome by the architect, sculptor, and painter Iacopo Barozzi, known as Vignola.

▲ The old Paço Episcopal now seat of the Museu Machado de Castro

The interior is a magnificent example of the Baroque, with a nave flanked by side chapels with *talha dourada* intarsias. The ceiling is a barrel vault and at the center of the transept is an immense dome. The retable on the high altar, seventeenth century *talha dourada*, has numerous statues and a splendid Mannerist painting of the *Nativity*. In the **Upper Choir** the two eighteenth century organs are of note.

The **Museu Machado de Castro** is housed in the old **Paço Episcopal**, the twelfth century bishop's palace built on the ruins of a first century B.C. Roman temple. The Museum contains an important collection of archaeological material such as the galleries of the Roman cryptoporticus, and one of the finest collections of medieval and Renaissance art in Portugal. Works by great artists of the school of Coimbra such as the *Virgin after the Annunciation* by Chanterène or the *Madonna and Child* and the statue of the *Knight* by the Portuguese master Mestre Pero (considered the genius of stone). There are also paintings of Portuguese and Flemish schools by artists such as Metsys with his *Ecce Homo*, and Isenbrandt or Ysenbrandt, Rembrandt and others. The sections devoted to jewellery, Oriental art and ceramics are also of note.

◄ Museu Machado de Castro, the Virgin by Nicolas Chanterène

◄ Museu Machado de Castro, Madonna and Child by the Portuguese artist Mestre Pero

▲ *View of the upper city with the Sé Nova seen from the University*

University

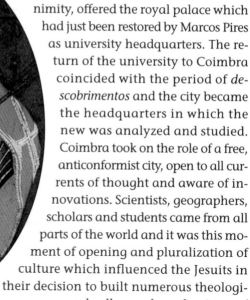

The Porta Férrea is the entrance to the temple of knowledge at **Paço das Escolas** (the university center), in the old royal palace on the Acropolis, from which a splendid panorama of the city and its river is also to be had. The University, *Estudo Geral*, was founded in Lisbon by King Dinis in 1290 and moved to Coimbra in 1308 and originally prepared young men for theological studies. After returning to Lisbon, it was definitively transferred to Coimbra in 1537. One of the first directors of the **College of Arts** was the Frenchman André de Resende and the king, with great magna-nimity, offered the royal palace which had just been restored by Marcos Pires as university headquarters. The return of the university to Coimbra coincided with the period of *descobrimentos* and the city became the headquarters in which the new was analyzed and studied. Coimbra took on the role of a free, anticonformist city, open to all currents of thought and aware of innovations. Scientists, geographers, scholars and students came from all parts of the world and it was this moment of opening and pluralization of culture which influenced the Jesuits in their decision to built numerous theological colleges where the rigors of the faith and doctrine could be taught to their students. This also played a part in the arrival of the Inquisition, and Coimbra (as well as Évora and Lisbon) was one of the capitals most active in the work of the ecclesiastical Tribunal. The Jesuits then took over the direction of the College of the Arts, the university. It was then thanks to the enlightened despot, the minister Marquês de Pombal, that the Jesuits were expelled from Portugal and the university was returned to its former state with a reform which made it possible to introduce human sciences and teaching by lay persons.

The **Porta Férrea**, a magnificent Renaissance portal decorated with columns and sculpture, leads into the **Pátio das Escolas**, the large courtyard on which the old faculty buildings face out. On the left of the portal is the building of the Jesuit

◄ *Paço das Escolas (the University) from the Cathedral*

college of **São Pedro**, while on the right is **Via Latina**, a gallery construction with columns and arches that support a triangular pediment, and two imposing flights of stairs on either side which lend it a certain monumentality. In Via Latina, so-called because this was where the students were required to speak only in Latin, and now the headquarters of the **Reitoria**, the offices and residence of the chancellor where academic ceremonies are held. In the **Sala dos Capelos** (Sala dos Grandes Actos) where the students once took their exams, now they only discuss their theses. The Hall, in red brocade, has its original wooden ceiling,

▲ *The Bell Tower and the entrance on Via Latina*

completely decorated, while the walls are lined with paintings of the kings of Portugal, and seventeenth century azulejos. Next to it is the **Sala do Exame Privado**, with the portraits of the university chancellors on the walls. The frescoed ceiling is a masterpiece by José Ferreira Araújo. The room has a **Varanda**, a balcony with a wrought iron railing, with a panorama of the entire city.

Symbol of the university is the **Bell Tower**, with three bells, visible from anywhere in Coimbra. The students have given a name to each bell which has a different sound: Cabra which marks the hours, Cabrão which is the wake-up bell in the morning (at seven) and which also rings at the end of each lecture, and Balão, the largest, which rings for funerals, and for graduation ceremonies. Next to the tower is the **Capela de São Miguel** – with a superb Manueline portal by Marcos Pires – which was begun around 1500. The interior is eighteenth century and it was João V, the "spendthrift" king, who had it covered with panels of polychrome azulejos with a Rococo organ. The **Museu de Arte Sacra** with its collections of wooden statues, liturgical hangings and vestments, sacred texts and donations to the university belongs to the Chapel.

◄ *The Porta Férrea, Renaissance portal decorated with columns and sculptures which leads to the University*

The acknowledged masterpiece of the university is the **Joanina Library**, the zenith of Lusitanian Baroque architecture. Built on the model of the Viennese library, it bears the name of the king who financed it, João V. He is remembered here with an emblem on the fine portal and a large portrait inside. The three large rooms painted respectively in green, gold and red lacquer, house the three hundred thousand books and three thousand manuscripts of philosophy, law, theology and literature. There is a profusion of fine wood, such as rosewood and ebony, in the three Baroque rooms, as well as fine marbles, gold ornaments, ceilings frescoed by António Simões Ribeiro and superb intarsias on the balconies, the furniture and the tables. The **Museums** of **Astronomy**, **Anthropology** and **Physics** are the pride of the university. The physics museum contains the famous "genius mechanism", an old device for measuring intelligence, of which it is the only example in Europe.

▼ *Via Latina*

▲ *Capela de São Miguel with its splendid Manueline por*

▲ *The Baroque Joanina Library*

The terraced **Botanical Gardens** is also part of the university. It was created by Pombal next to the old **Aqueduto de São Sebastião** right behind the university. The eighteenth century park stretches out for twenty hectares and is open to the public only a few hours each day. It contains many species of rare trees and plants, and above all a great variety of tropical plants.

From the park, continuing our walk, we descend towards **Praça da República**, a delightful modern square also known as Square of the Students, with an avenue that leads to the Baixa. Across the Mondego River with the new quarters, is the old female convent **Mosteiro de Santa Clara-a-Velha** founded in the fourteenth century by Queen Isabel, wife of King Dinis, who later became Saint Elizabeth (Isabel) of Portugal. The convent, closed for many years because of floods, contained the tomb of the queen. Her remains were moved to the other seventeenth century **Convento de Santa Clara-a-Nova**,

▲ *Panorama of the lower c* *and the Convento de Santa Clara-a-No*

▼ *The Botanical Gardens created by the Marquês de Pombal*

now mostly occupied by the army. In the **Church** with its nave and two aisles, dedicated to the queen, is the precious *Tomb of Saint Isabel*, in silver, by Teixeira Lopes. There are also numerous paintings and wooden panels with scenes from the *Life of the Saint-Queen*. It is said that the queen wanted to distribute bread to the poor and was reproved by her husband, the king, who frowned on his wife's charitable behavior. There is also a wooden statue of the saint-queen, in the habit of the Poor Clares, which is celebrated with a great religious festival every two years, on July 4, and is carried in procession through the city during the **Festa da Rainha Santa**.

Still two things must be seen before leaving Coimbra, both near the old convent of Santa Clara. One will appeal partic-

122

▲ Convento de Santa Clara-a-Nova

► La Rainha Santa Isabel, painting by Nuno Gonçalves
in the Museu de Arte Antiga in Lisbon

ularly to the children, the **Portugal dos Pequenitos**, a large amusement park where Salazar had all the monuments of Portugal and the typical dwellings of Portugal and the former colonies reproduced in miniature. The other more romantic one regards Inês de Castro, killed as a result of intrigues of love: the **Quinta das Lágrimas.** The splendid gardens of the old palace now a luxurious hotel, where tradition has it that Inês, whom the Infante Pedro was in love with, was killed by the hired killers of his father, King Afonso IV, can be visited. It is said that on the site of this horrible crime a spring bubbled forth, the **Fonte dos Amores**. It subsequently became a place where all lovers made eternal vows.

► The Fonte dos Amores in the Quinta das Lágrimas

View of the Parco Portugal dos Pequenitos

Pedro and Inês: love beyond the tomb

▲ Facade of the old palace of Quinta das Lágrimas, now a luxury hotel

Ever since the fourteenth century the moving story has been told in Portugal of Pedro I, son of Afonso IV, and Inês de Castro, a lovely young noble girl from Galicia, and of their ill-starred love. The infante Pedro I, heir to the throne of Lusitania, fell head over heels in love with the fascinating Inês. For reasons of state his father forced him to marry Costança, an older princess. But Inês and Pedro continued to see each other in secret. Costança died after the birth of the heir Fernando, and Pedro, who had secretly married Inês in Bragança, decided to move with his army to Coimbra, despite the opposition of his father.

King Afonso IV, who feared for the Portuguese kingdom in this union with Inês from Galicia, decided to do away with his beautiful daughter in law while his son was out hunting. It was the 7th of January, 1355. Inês de Castro was walking in the gardens of the Quinta das Lágrimas in Coimbra when the assassins struck. Two years later, when his father died and Pedro became king, he finally succeeded in revenging this dastardly deed and killed the murderers and ate their hearts.

He then had the body of Inês exhumed and placed on one of two thrones in the monastery of Santa Clara. She was dressed in regal apparel and in an extravagant but rather macabre ceremony Inês was crowned queen and the court dignitaries were forced to kiss her bony hand.

King Pedro governed the country for ten years (1357-1367) and then had two sumptuous richly decorated Gothic tombs built which are now in the Cathedral of Alcobaça. The Life of Saint Bartholomew, Pedro's patron saint who was flayed alive, is sculptured in the aedicules.

When Pedro died, the two lovers were buried facing each other so that when the trumpets of the Last Judgment sounded and the dead were resurrected, they would already be together. In his Os Lusíadas, Luís de Camões dedicated immortal lines to the sad story of the two lovers, who became the symbol of that eternal love so dear to poets and writers.

QUINTA DAS LÁGRIMAS
As filhas do Mondego a morte escura
Longo tempo chorando memoraram,
E, por memória eterna, em fonte pura
As lágrimas choradas transformaram.
O nome lhe puseram, que inda dura,
Dos amores de Inês, que ali passaram.
Vede que fresca fonte rega as flores,
Que lágrimas são a água e o nome Amores.
Luís de Camões Os Lusíadas cant. III, est. CXXXV.

▶ The tombs of King Pedro and of Inês, in the Mosteiro di Alcobaça

FIGUEIRA DA FOZ

This port city is also a popular vacation site with modern and luxurious hotels and tourist facilities where visitors can relax, enjoy themselves and practice sports. There's also a casino which opens at three in the afternoon and closes at dawn.

Figueira da Foz is a lively pleasure-loving sun-drenched city, a happy place where you live well and the number of winter tourists is annually increasing. The city, with its twenty-five thousand inhabitants, is located at the mouth of the Mondego River (hence its name, *Foz*, or mouth) with the promontory of eucalyptus trees and pines, the Serra da Boa Viagem which protects it from the winds, behind. It is only thirty five kilometers from Coimbra. The splendid beach with its fine white sand, the *Praia da Claridade* (luminosity) which bears witness to the name, is over three kilometers long and every year attracts vaca-

▲ *Gulls at the mouth of the Mondego River*

Figueira da Foz and the beach with its fine white sand

▲ Small fishing boats

▶ Sardine catch

tioners and surfers who accept the challenge of the great waves (in a storm they can be over ten meters high) of the Ocean. In 1996 the city hosted the world surfing championship.

The seaside promenade is flanked by small geometrically aligned old houses almost all the same height painted white with blue and yellow stripes.

In Portugal Figueira da Foz is also well known for the large quantities of cod and sardines fished here, as well as for its oysters, even though most of them come from commercial oyster beds. Not infrequently women can be encountered near the port putting out cod to dry on metal bars.

Tourism, fishing and agriculture (with great stretches of corn fields and rice paddies in the countryside) are what Figueira da Foz lives on. The city owes its de-velopment and its fortunes to the silting up of the port of Aveiro. The relics in the **Museu Municipal Santos Rocha** show that it was originally nothing but a small fishing village at the mouth of the river.

The triangular sixteenth century **Forte de Santa Catarina** dominates the mouth of the river there where it meets the Ocean and where the city then built the Bairro Novo, the new residential quarter with luxurious mansions, pedestrian streets and hotels. The Fort was the headquarters of the famous Duke of Wellington who fought with his ten thousand English soldiers side by side with the Portuguese in the peninsular war against Napoleon. In the city center, nothing remains of the old **Convento de Santo António** founded in 1527 but the **Igreja da Misericórdia** with its frescoes of the *Life of the Saint* on the walls.

Buarcos is the fishermen's quarter with its ancient medieval walls and where modernization has still not caught up. Here Nature offers one of its most imposing and fascinating sights - the Ocean itself. It can even be enjoyed sitting in a restaurant or a smoky *adega* before a dish of the traditional fisherman's cuisine, such as the *Caldeirada de petingas*, one of the tastiest and most delicate fish soups, made with the small sardines, or an exquisite *Cabrito assado à regional* (roast kid).

◀ The many-colored houses

CONTENTS